AF291344

The Practice – What Moves Artists

On Making Less
Rirkrit Tiravanija

On Making Less
Rirkrit Tiravanija

Jenny Schlenzka & Julia Grosse (editors)

Berliner Festspiele / Gropius Bau
Bierke Verlag

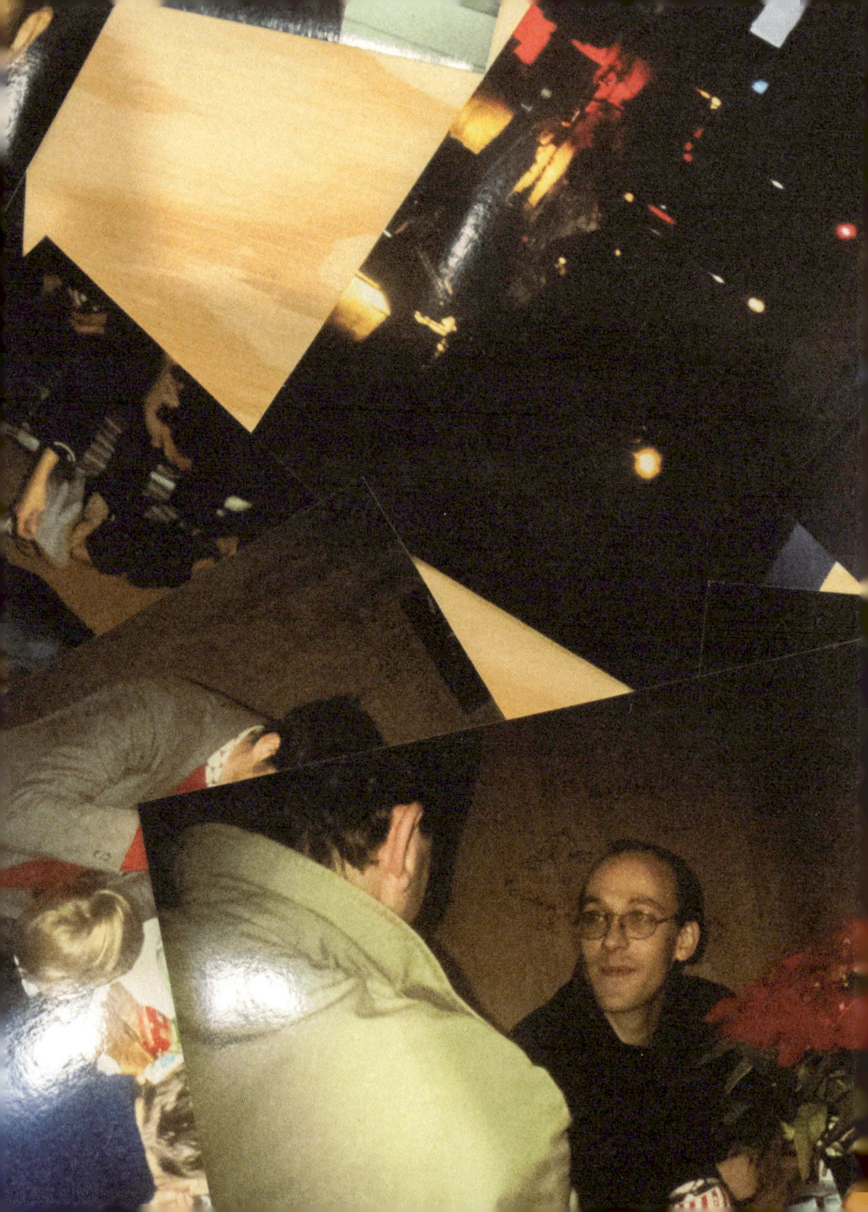

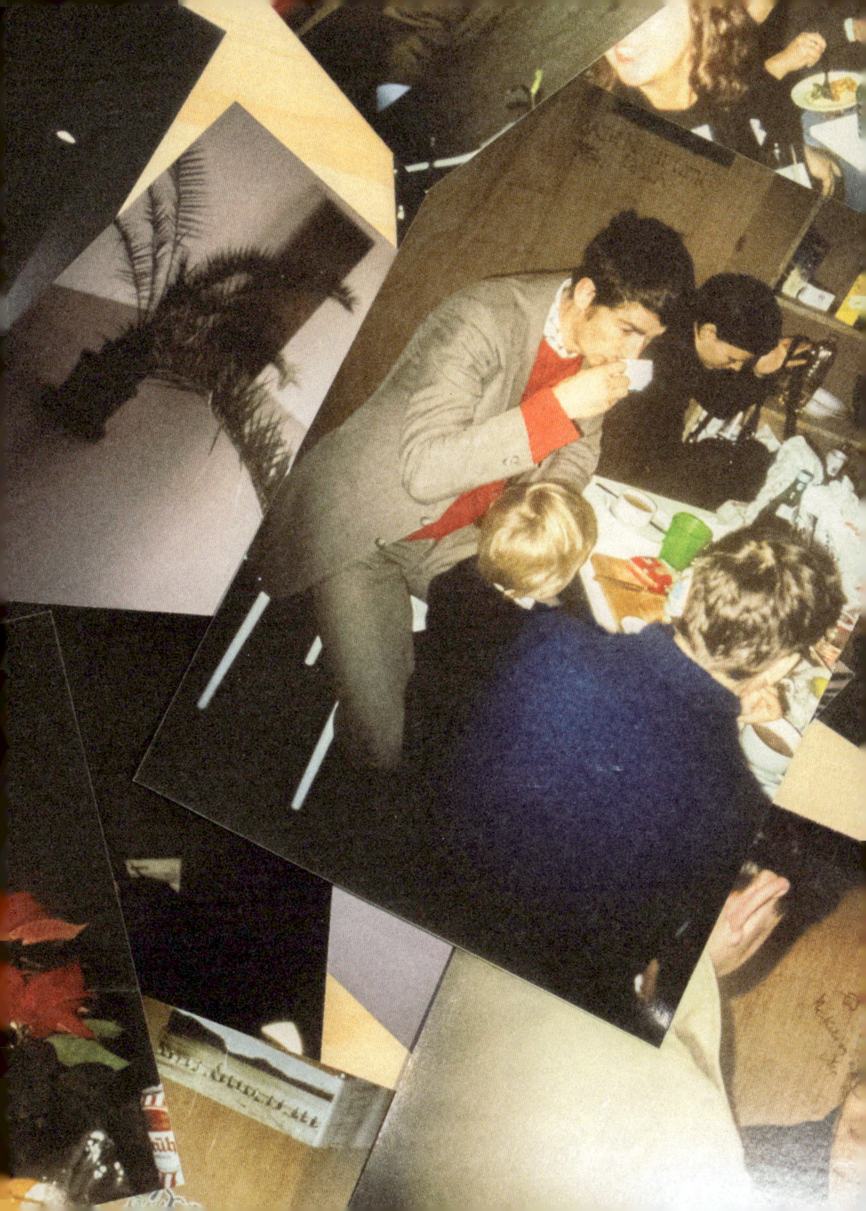

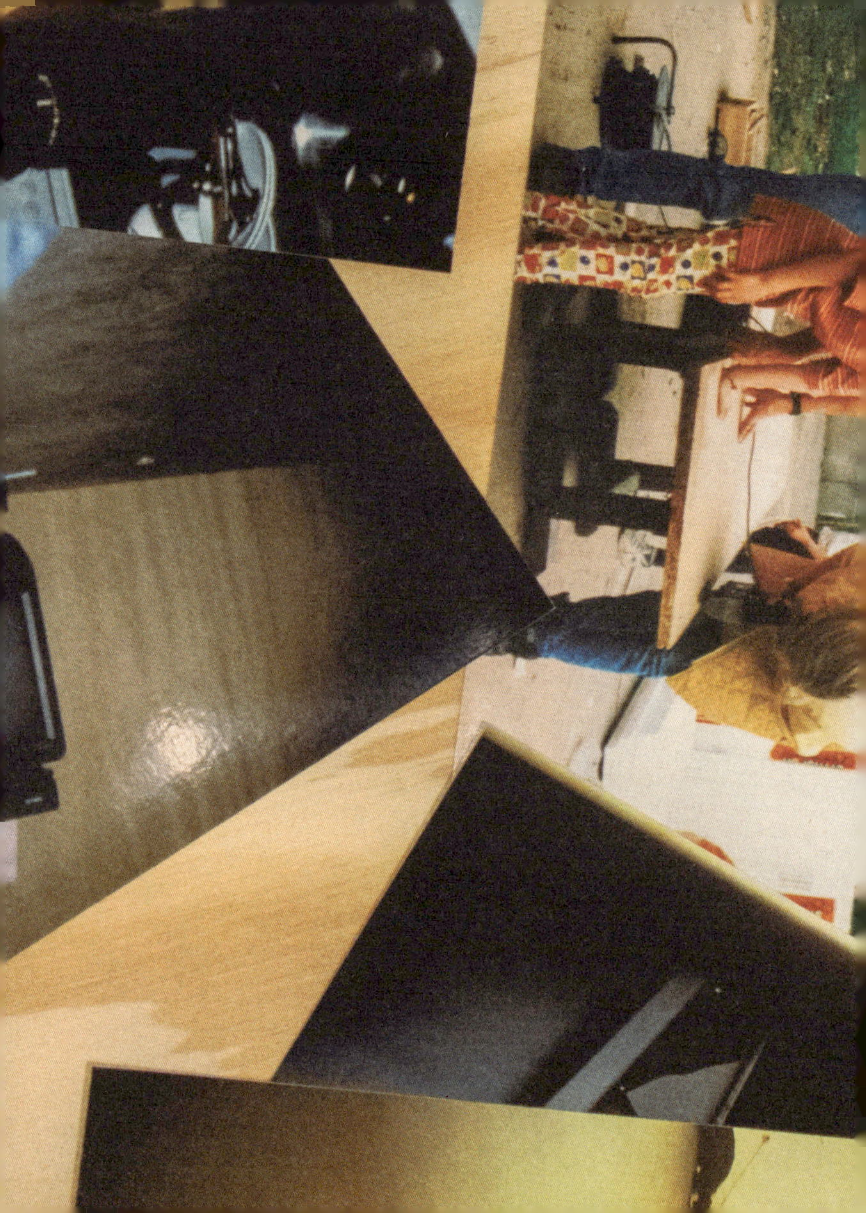

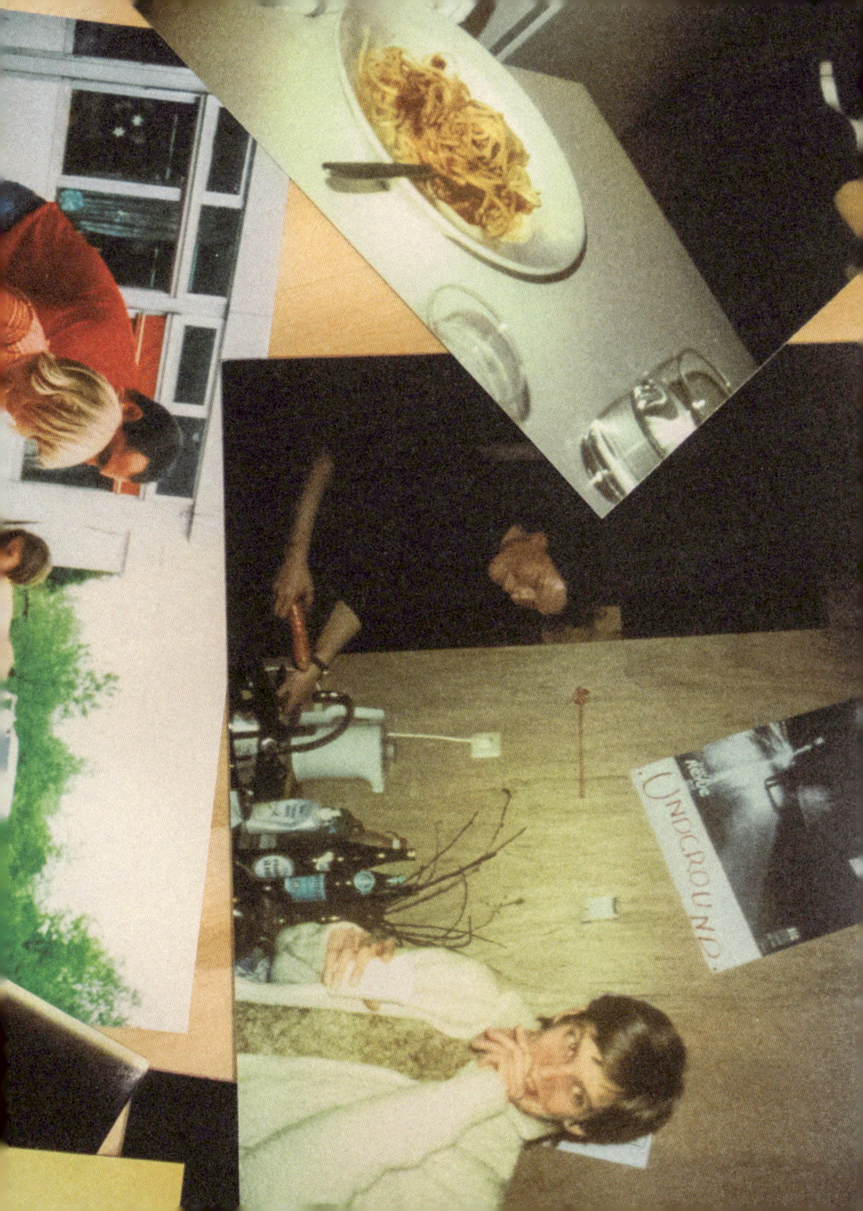

A DIFFERENT KIND OF NOTHING

Untitled, (free)   1992

divert attention away from the anticipated act
the production of a creative act, the production of an idea
negation of an act
Activity
remove all the doors from its frame   open up
remove the office in to the exhibition space
remove the exhibition space
Site/ non site
exhibition space as site   other space as non site
site specificity
remove myself from the position of authorship
remove myself from the exhibition
remove myself from production
remove myself
cook some food and eat it
because it fills empty stomach

I would rather (br)**eat**(h) than make art

what is obvious here
(1)   the subversion of art and commerce
(2)   the subversion of authority (figures)
(C)   the subversion of the gallery going public
(D)   the lack of idea
(5)   the lack of talent
(6)   the lack of social political concerns
(7)   the space is diffrent
(8)   the smell is diffrent
(9)   the food is diffrent
(10) not much is happening
(11) does not do anything
(12) nothing new
(14) its been done much better much longer
(15) its art
(16) its art in the disguise of life
(17) its life trying hard to be art
(18) can't even talk about it because it has no relevence
(19) why bother
(20) Allan Kaprow
(21) Flxus
(22) Joseph Beuys
(23) Happenings
(24) Event
(25) Speorri
(26) Robert Morris
(27) Gordon Matta Clark
(28) may be even Duchamp
(29) its a Marxist critique
(30) its an environmental statement

(31) its garbage
(32) its delicious
(33) its too spicy
(34) what is there to sell
(35) its just a spectecle
(36) its a spectecle
(37) what does it mean
(38) its poetic
(39) its metaphorical
(40) its meta
(41) its too obvious

free
free bee
free base
free dom
free form
free agent
free time
free will
free way
free ticket
free food
free speech
free slavery
free Tibet
free Cypruss
free Palestine
free East Timor
free Scottland
free school
free health care
free sex
free mind from body
free state
free chequing
free to be co opted
free from anxiety
free from commitment
free from birth
free from emotions
free from desires
free of influences
free activities
free love
free to travel
free choice
free beer

free to live
free to shop
free opportunity
free fall
free wheeling
free membership
free homes
free woman
free copy
free from growth
free of MSG
free radio
free press
free of fat
free condoms
free medicine
free contraception
free needles
free party
free from oppression
free for all

What is it that we are trying to do beyound that which has already
be accomplished by history. How can we critique that which is
critical. In the image of the snake eating its own tail.
Always trying to move ahead of conciousness, trying to reestablish
itself as history. The race with time.
The 100 meter sprint gold medalist at the olympic does more to
change the world and history in under ten seconds.
Ahead of itself, measured in gold, weighing in critical value
a semblence of history is made.
History as in Western history. The Occidental.

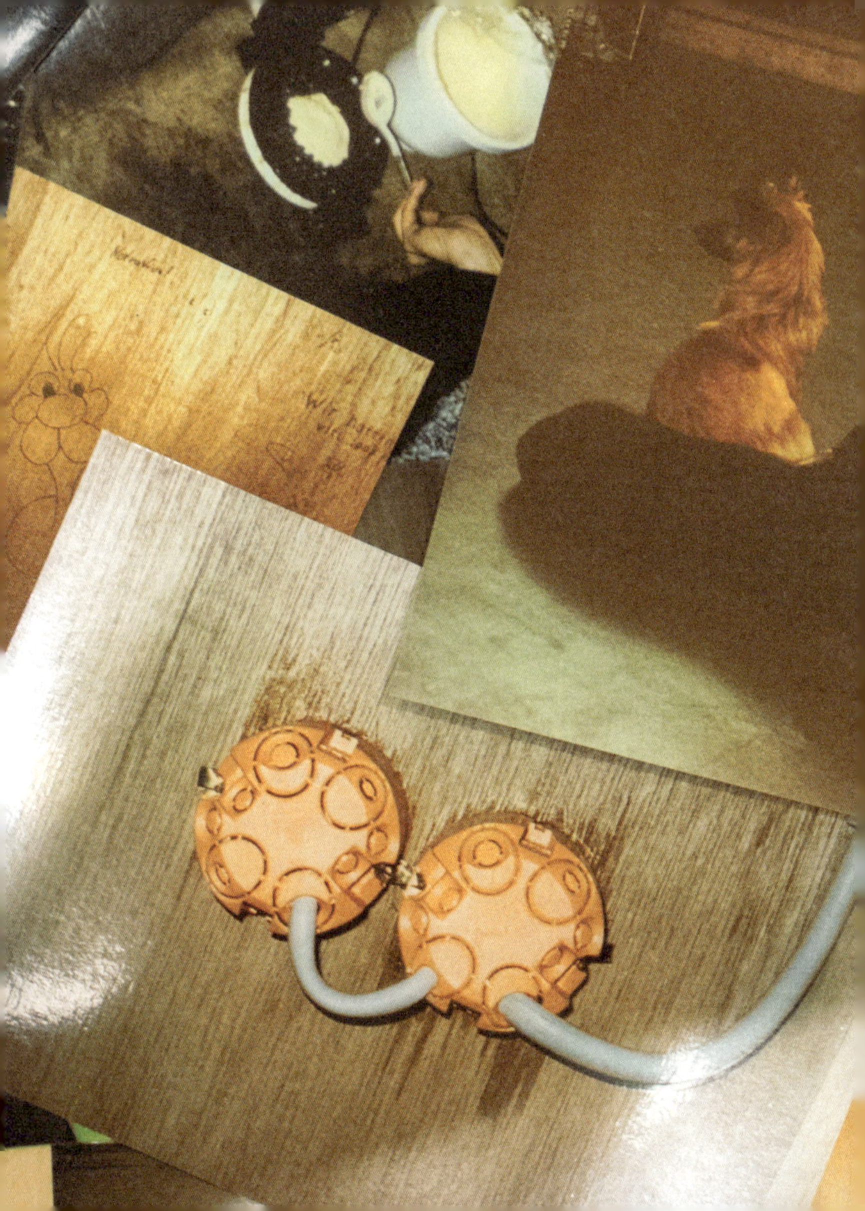

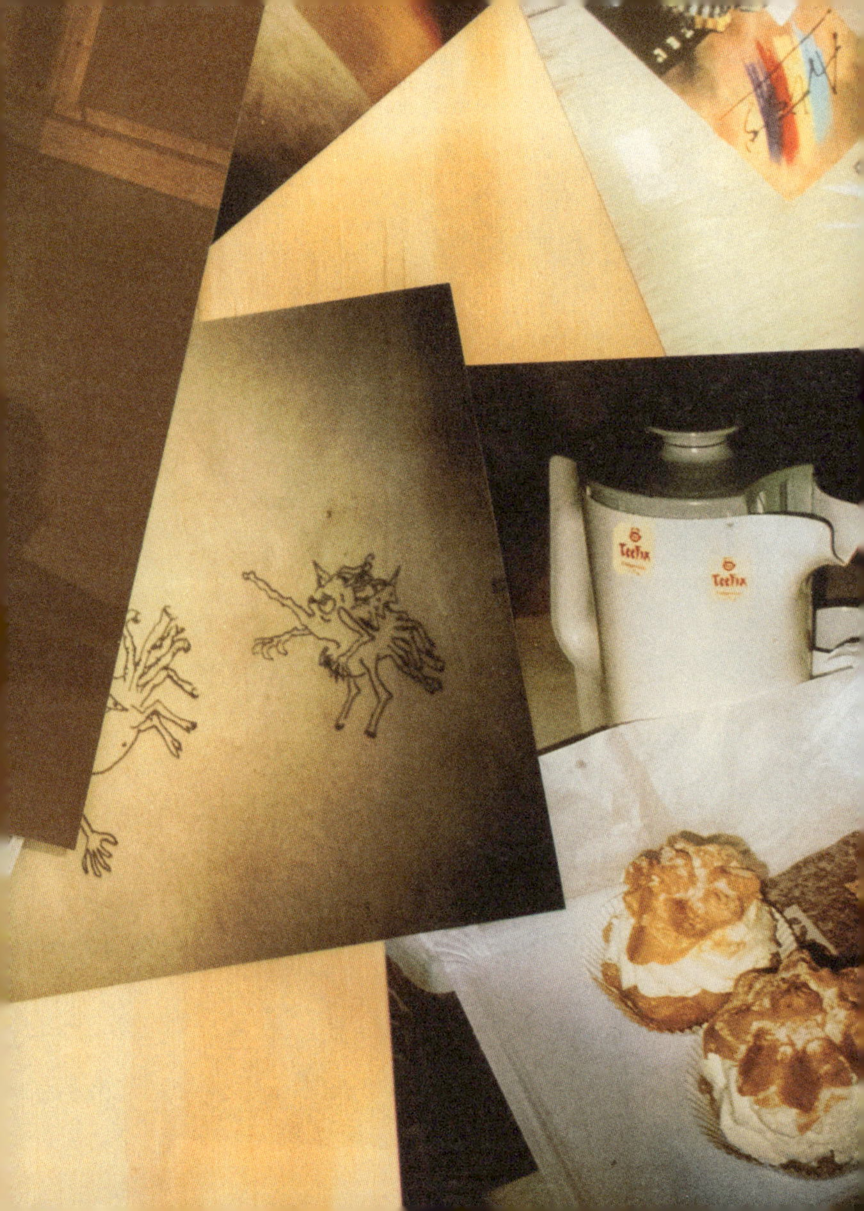

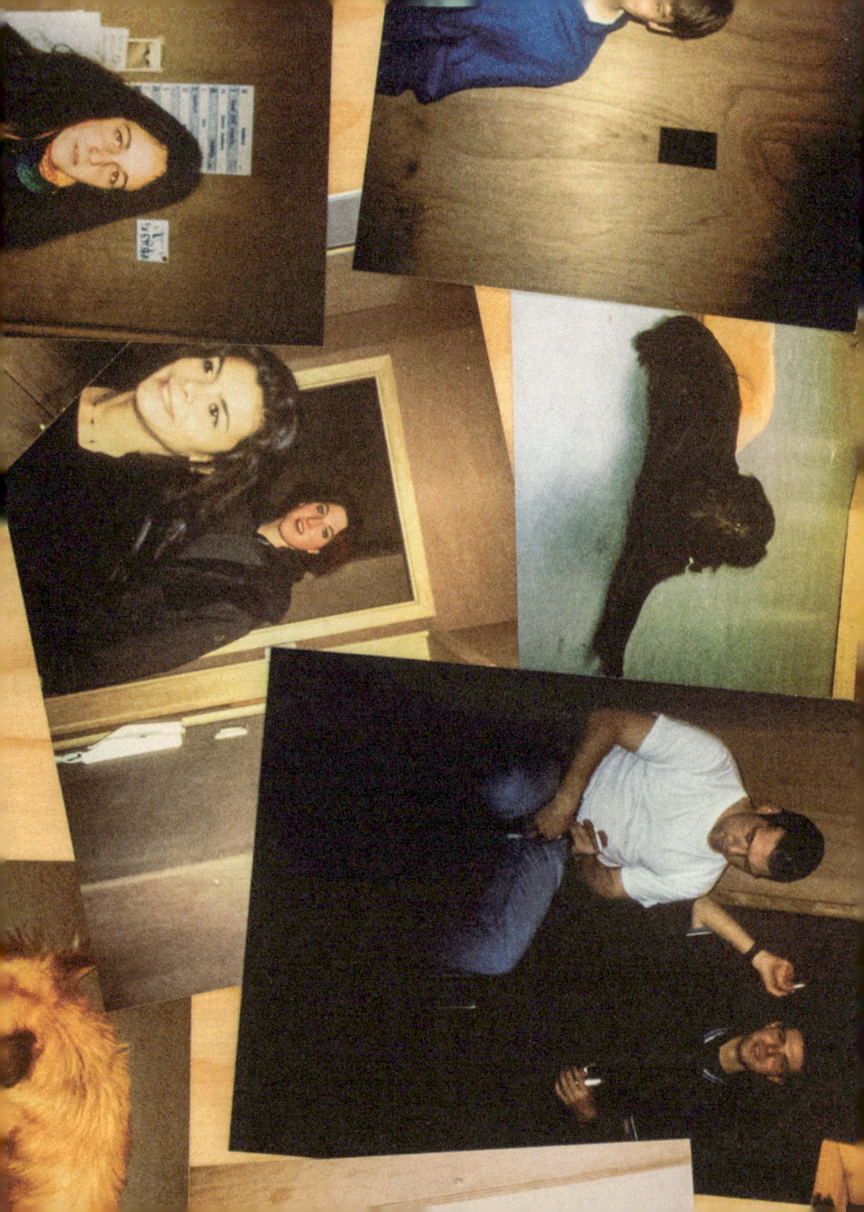

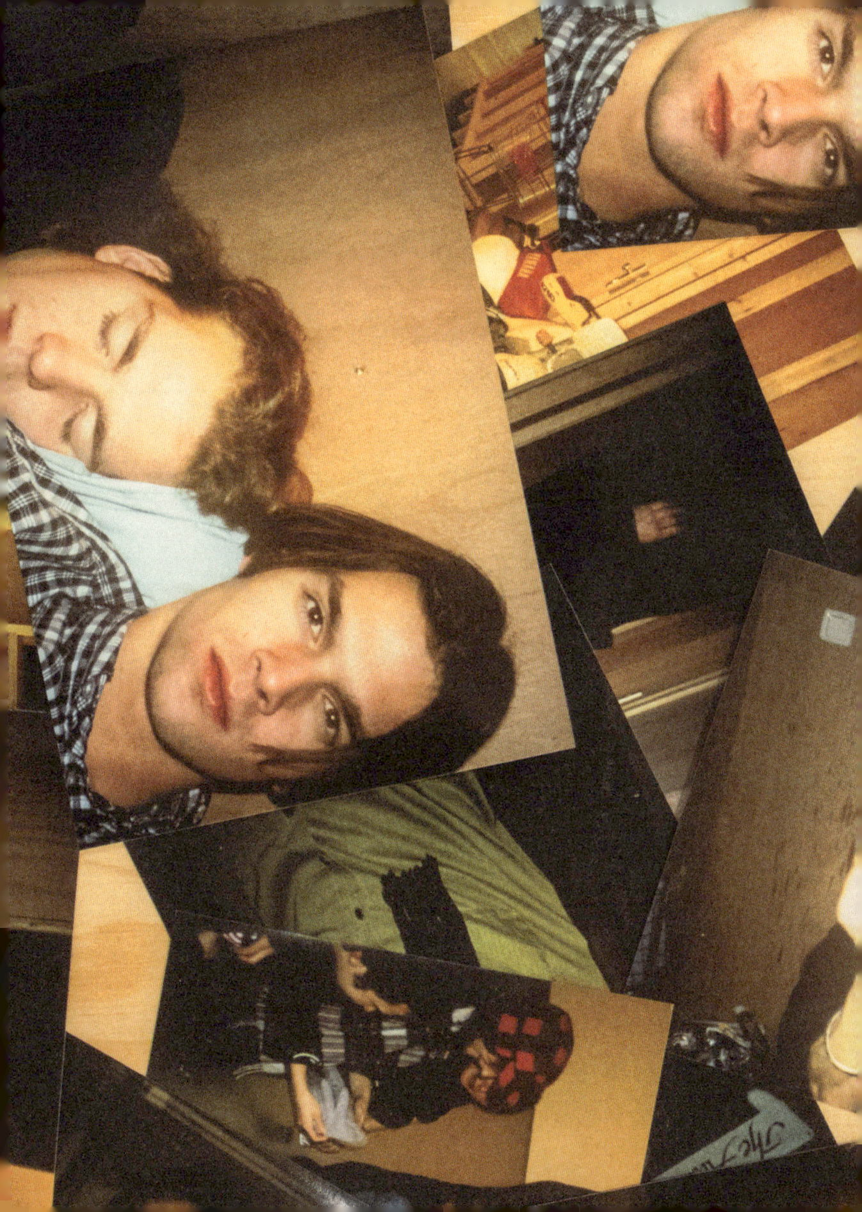

ON MAKING LESS

A conversation between Rirkrit Tiravanija,
Jenny Schlenzka & Julia Grosse
Berlin, 12 September 2024

<u>Julia Grosse</u>: In our initial conversation about this book, you said that you are interested in the idea of making less, of not doing anything as a practice. And your work is known for creating situations that people can participate in, where they can do something: they eat, they drink, they play music or ping pong. You build platforms for people to use. Your way of making less leads to people doing a lot!

<u>Rirkrit Tiravanija</u>: Yes, it's definitely a lot of work not to do anything!

Jenny Schlenzka: You have been teaching Fine Arts at Columbia University for more than 20 years. How do you teach in a "do-nothing" way?

Rirkrit Tiravanija: There's no method. When I make a platform it's not that I know how people should use it. I can only say: here is a piece of wood on the floor, which is a platform. You can use it, or you can use it by not using it. You have to step over the line yourselves. Or if you'd rather follow the line that other people make, then you can also think about why you're following it. It's interesting, especially as an artist in the role of a professor, trying *not* to make the students follow you. But you're still kind of teaching them. When people say "This and that person is a student of Beuys!" then they think that this student obviously follows the practice of Beuys. But my lesson from Beuys would be *not* to do what Beuys does. I'm trying to teach people to be themselves. I'm not even trying to teach them to become artists.

Julia Grosse: In recent years, discourse around restitution has gained more public attention, debating and more often also meeting the demands to return looted artefacts obtained via colonial routes that are held in Western museum collections. In 1987, you had commented on the Southeast Asian collection of the Art Institute of Chicago, where you studied. You created a text work that says, "WE DEMAND THE RETURN OF OUR CULTURAL ARTIFACTS IN THE MUSEUM OF THE ART INSTITUTE OF CHICAGO. OTHERWISE WE WILL BLOW IT UP."* What were you aiming at with that work?

Rirkrit Tiravanija: Well, coincidentally there was a big restitution case of the Vishnu lintel around the same time. Demands were made for it to be returned from the Chicago Art Institute to the Thai government in the 1980s. The months after I had made the text work, Thai people came and protested at the Art Institute of Chicago,

* Rirkrit Tiravanija, *untitled 1987 (text in red and black)*.

because there was a piece from the temple that was taken away. But for me, the work not only has to do with restitution. Because in the end it's really against Western knowledge production, which is based on collecting. The West is collecting so that it has whatever it thinks is important and then because it collects it can name it and catalogue it. And so I would like to kind of point to that and say: return it to life!

<u>Jenny Schlenzka</u>: So another form of making less!

<u>Rirkrit Tiravanija</u>: Return the artefacts to life! It's like saying: Stop collecting and start living! Or: Stop taking pictures and just look with your eyes!

<u>Julia Grosse</u>: You once mentioned that another artist advised you to not make art for one year. Did you follow the advice and what did you do and not do that year?

Rirkrit Tiravanija: Yes, I was still a young artist then, I was making sculptural things and I was fairly successful at that. We were just sitting on top of a mountain in Banff, Canada, just me and him on a rock and he said: Stop Making Art. And of course, this is something a lot of art teachers say to students as a provocation, because you need to trip them up a little. And I think that really was important to me. I wasn't so much following the advice, but more trying to find out what it means to stop making art.

Jenny Schlenzka: And what happened?

Rirkrit Tiravanija: You stop thinking in a certain way, and then you are more open and free. I say this to my students: Once you decide to be an artist, it doesn't matter what you do – you're always an artist. It's just about that little thought that you are thinking, it's just the attitude of how you live and how you think about living. So to be an artist is maybe just to think differently about how everything is and how the world thinks of itself.

<u>Jenny Schlenzka</u>: Do you remember the moment when you decided to become an artist?

<u>Rirkrit Tiravanija</u>: Yeah, the moment when I saw Kazimir Malevich's *White on White* and the ready-made *Fountain* by Marcel Duchamp. It wasn't even that I decided to be an artist, because I didn't even know what this is, an artist. It was more like, oh this is a really interesting idea and I need to know more. When I was interested in Duchamp, I realised Duchamp talks about chance – it's like gambling, like tossing the dice. Even more than that, it was John Cage's idea of silence, which is never silent*. Silence is also that same idea of not making anything, but you are still doing silence.

Through Cage I understood that we [in Thailand] have been living this way all along. In fact I would

* *4'33"* was a "silent piece" from 1952 by experimental composer John Cage lasting four minutes and thirty-three seconds in which the score instructs performers not to play their instruments.

say I don't have to do all the things that John
Cage does, because I already live it.

<u>Julia Grosse</u>: You once said, "I don't make things
unless I have to" and one could certainly understand this approach as a very sustainable way
of living. Could you talk a little bit about this
aspect of sustainability in your practice?

<u>Rirkrit Tiravanija</u>: In the end, personally, if I did
not have to do anything I would live on very little,
because I don't have big desires. I want to live
better; maybe that is a desire. Maybe I want
to have an electric car rather than one that runs
on fossil fuel, which in the end is also a huge
contradiction because it's just as unsustainable,
and probably you should just walk. When I travel
back to upstate New York, where I live, I could
just not do anything, because in the end that's
the most sustainable way.

People always still want to see the thing and don't understand that it's about the doing…

Julia Grosse: How do things reappear over the years in your exhibition making? Is the original important to you?

Rirkrit Tiravanija: It's more this idea of using things. It's kind of like a pot. If you have it, you use it, and if it breaks, you get a new one. But it's not a particular pot. And it's not a particular curry. It's more about the person doing it. People always still want to see the thing and don't understand that it's about the doing. There is no need for any original thing, no need for the authenticity, because it's about the action. The action is what is "authentic," if you will (for lack of a better word). And then it should always change, because when you do the same action and you do it from one day to the next it has already changed so there is no need to try to do the exact same thing every day.

<u>Julia Grosse</u>: For this book you suggested reprinting an excerpt from the famous 1970s book
The One-Straw Revolution by Masanobu Fukuoka, in which he is arguing for a "do-nothing agricultural method" without fertiliser and insecticide, where the farmer allows things to just evolve. In places, the book sounds a little rigid by today's standards, condemning modern medicine, etc.

<u>Rirkrit Tiravanija</u>: I think it was not only that. It's really against Western thinking. When he says medicine, he means Western medicine. The old medicine is much more holistic. I think also in terms of agriculture the book is against industrialised agriculture. What I like about him is the fact that for him, it is more about observation. Whatever you do, you're just spending time looking and you study. For instance, how the spider makes its web and how the spider spends its time living – that tells you all these other things. In connection to this I could talk about fly fishing, which I like doing. Because fly fishing is not about catching fish. It's about studying nature. When

you do fly fishing, you're not actually fishing; but you present the fly to the fish and it is through this specific movement that you can cast the lure lightly onto the water. And if you don't present it so that it looks real, the fish will never eat it.

<u>Jenny Schlenzka</u>: Again, it's about observation.

<u>Rirkrit Tiravanija</u>: Yes. When I'm telling students not to do a lot, it's because I want them to spend more time looking before they do anything. But of course, they have to look around themselves, because it's their time and their space. I do everything in my head so that I don't have to do it until it actually has to happen. This is very economical. I say to my students, turn a picture into language. You can talk about it, describe it with your words. I think you have to be able to describe the work before you make it.

Jenny Schlenzka: Is there a difference for you between doing less and making less?

Rirkrit Tiravanija: I mean, there's already things done, right? And it could continue to be done. And so doing less is like not making more. When I left the exhibition halls empty in the museum retrospective in Rotterdam in 2004,* this was as good as I could do it. It's an empty room – there's nothing there and you can activate it yourself and then something happens! I'm trying to find different ways to not do things. I used to say if I had all the answers, I would stop. And I haven't really stopped yet.

* In the retrospective at Museum Boijmans Van Beuningen in Rotterdam from 4 December 2004 to 6 February 2005, Rirkrit Tiravanija build plywood replicas of seven past exhibitions and left those spaces empty. Guides and wall labels provided visitors with information on the works he had shown there.

<u>Jenny Schlenzka</u>: May we press you about some contradictions, which we know is a very Western thing to do? How do you reconcile the fact you're saying you don't want to create anything and yet there are two large shows of your work in the world right now; the one that originated at MoMA PS1 in New York and ours in Berlin.

<u>Rirkrit Tiravanija</u>: Well, I would say that it's possible to have these two large retrospective shows of my work happening at the same time exactly because there are no real objects. You can remake it; you can redo it. So in that sense there is, but there isn't. There isn't a need to actually bring the original over here.

Jenny Schlenzka: Your work *untitled 1995 (bon voyage monsieur ackermann)*, a yellow Opel Commodore, with which you and Franz Ackermann drove through all of Europe?
You couldn't easily redo that car.

Rirkrit Tiravanija: True, but then we would have done the show without the car. But you know, there's also the other thing: These shows are each very different, they are curated. It's the desire of someone. It's not how I would do it.

Jenny Schlenzka: Maybe another contradiction about you wanting to make, create, or do less: It seems like you never say no to any suggested project or exhibition. Don't you have to be able to say no to do less?

Rirkrit Tiravanija: Again, it's like silence. There is never silence. Doing less is still doing. It's not like not doing. And when I'm saying that I'm doing a lot less myself, it might mean that someone else is doing a lot more.

<u>Jenny Schlenzka</u>: It's remarkable how much you reference Western art and that you say wanting to become an artist came from Duchamp and Malevich. In which way would you say you need the *other* as well?

<u>Rirkrit Tiravanija</u>: Yes, you need the *other* to understand yourself. There is this funny idea of artists "inventing" things. Picasso was appropriating objects from African contexts as material for his works. I am looking at the other to understand myself. When I was in Thailand, we always looked at the West. We always thought that's where we wanted to go. And then, once I went, I realised it's the same sunset – it's not like a better sunset and there are just as many problems.

You just need to
understand that
there is a gap
and that gap has
to be accepted
in order to
accept yourself

Julia Grosse: You recently talked about making
pottery as something that keeps you away
from doing art. Can you elaborate on what you
mean by being distracted from your practice
as an artist?

Rirkrit Tiravanija: Yes, weirdly it comes back to
the beginning, which is the desire to not have
the object. I mean making pottery is like fishing
or cooking – a space where I think. I am making
things that would be used.

Julia Grosse: You once said "In the East where I come from, one values the life around the object more than the object itself." So do we need a shift from objects to processes in art institutions?

Rirkrit Tiravanija: There is a gap of understanding. And that gap will always be there. But what you need to understand is that you don't even need to fill it or to try to fill it, you just need to understand that there *is* a gap and that gap has to be accepted in order to accept yourself. A lot of people still want to fill it, because of course they can't live with the gap. I mean I started off wanting to fill the gap. I cooked Pad Thai and did everything else. But it's not possible, you cannot fill it.

<u>Julia Grosse</u>: This idea of filling the gap and this idea of collecting as an accumulation of value, which is also an attempt to fill a gap, made us wonder whether you collect and if yes, what?

<u>Rirkrit Tiravanija</u>: Over the years I have accumulated a lot of old newspapers and other printed matter. But I would not call this a collection, the practice of keeping and reading them is in expectation of reuse. But you are right, I never thought I would have an archive, because I thought I don't want to keep anything. But by now I have a huge archive.* All the things that needed to go somewhere.

* Since 2009, art historian Jörn Schafaff and archivist Jan Pfeiffer have developed a classification system and database with over 30,000 archival records to date documenting 40 years of Tiravanija's work. The physical archive, located in Berlin, holds smaller works and multiples, as well as image, film and video material, correspondences, press, publications, a reference library and other extensive forms of documentation.

Julia Grosse: How do you explain the fact that despite your focus on openness and process in your work and your rejection of art objects, you still have a very distinct formal language?

Rirkrit Tiravanija: I know how to make art. I know how to make it, because I know the expectation of others who are looking at it and I can deal with that. I say to my students, you are just trying to do the thing that everyone is expecting of you. But to find yourself is to see that those expectations are not everything.

If we were in a better place
I would definitely just go
into the garden and not do
anything.

Jenny Schlenzka: Do you ever think about quitting art?

Rirkrit Tiravanija: In a way I have quit already, but I leave some signs on the road. Partly because we are still not in a better place. So I leave some footprints. If we were in a better place today, I would definitely just go into the garden and not do anything.

But we try to make alternative structures. An example is The Land Foundation we founded in Thailand. This was a piece of land that was to be cultivated.* Rice is grown there and the harvest is shared by all participants involved and donated to some families in the local village. Then artists are invited there to bring in their practice, like the

* The Land Foundation was co-founded by Rirkrit Tiravanija and Kamin Lertchaiprasert in 1998 in a rice field near Chiang Mai, Thailand, as a community-run farm, an architectural site, an artists' retreat and residency and an experiment for alternative ecological and economic models. https://www.thelandfoundation.org/about

group Superflex from Copenhagen developed
the idea of "supergas" there (utilising biomass
to produce gas for the kitchen stove and lamps).
These kinds of collaborative projects were what
we thought was needed for the younger people
in that area and they are still needed. I think for
me, it's more about making platforms in different
contexts. It doesn't even have to be art.

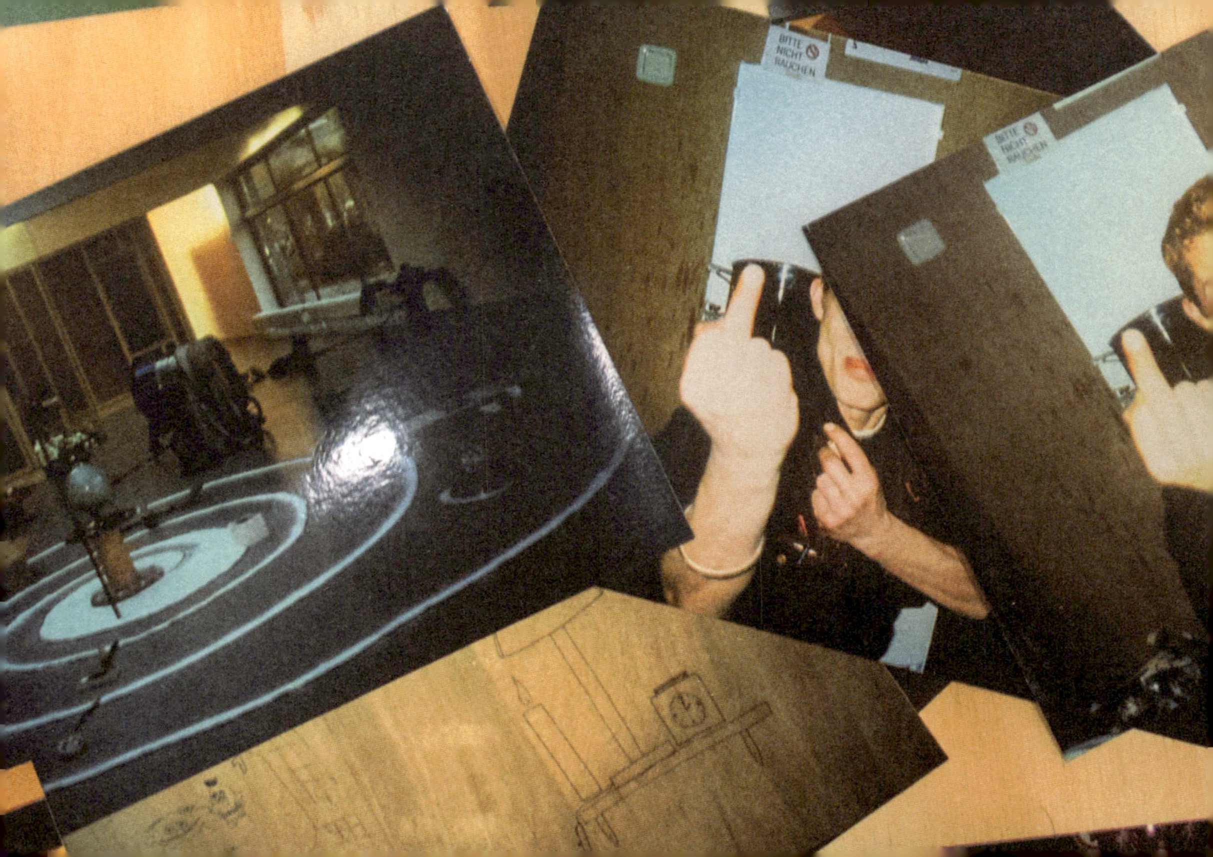
BITTE
NICHT
RAUCHEN

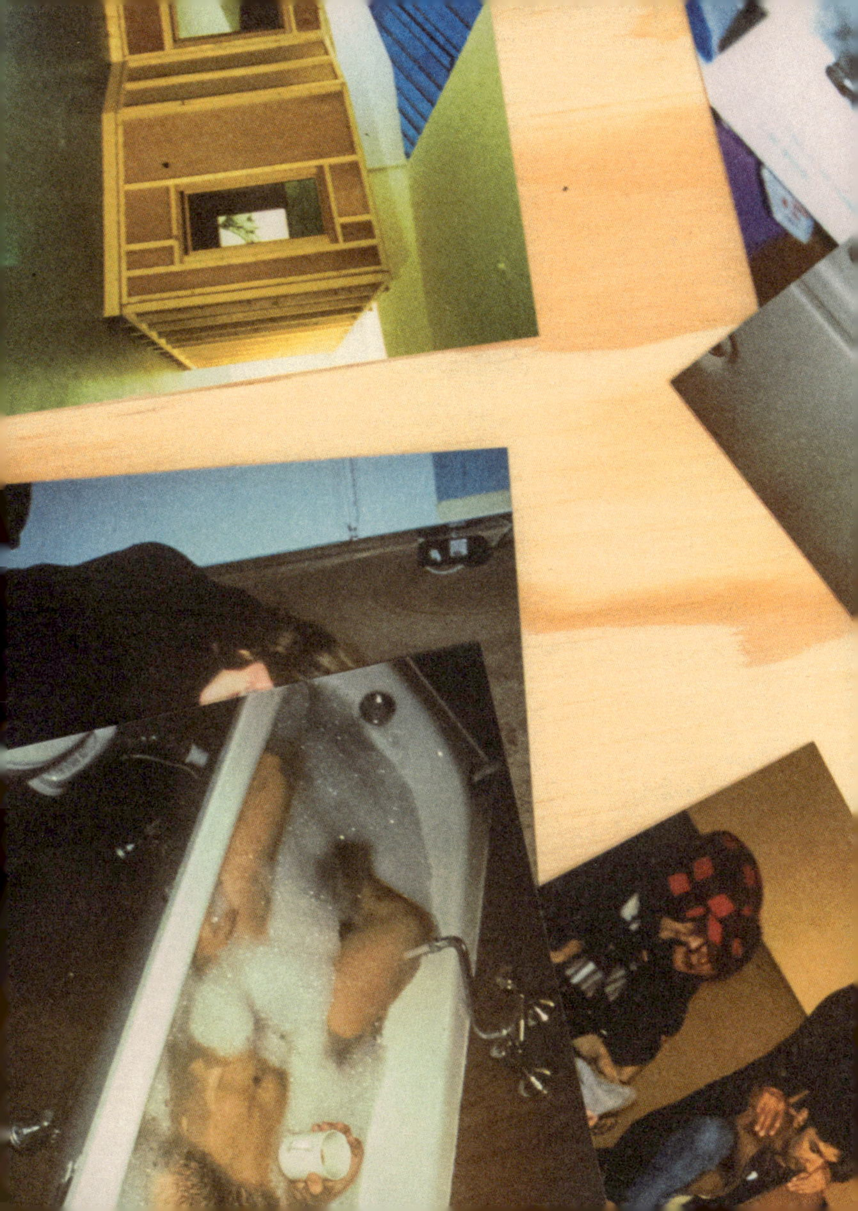

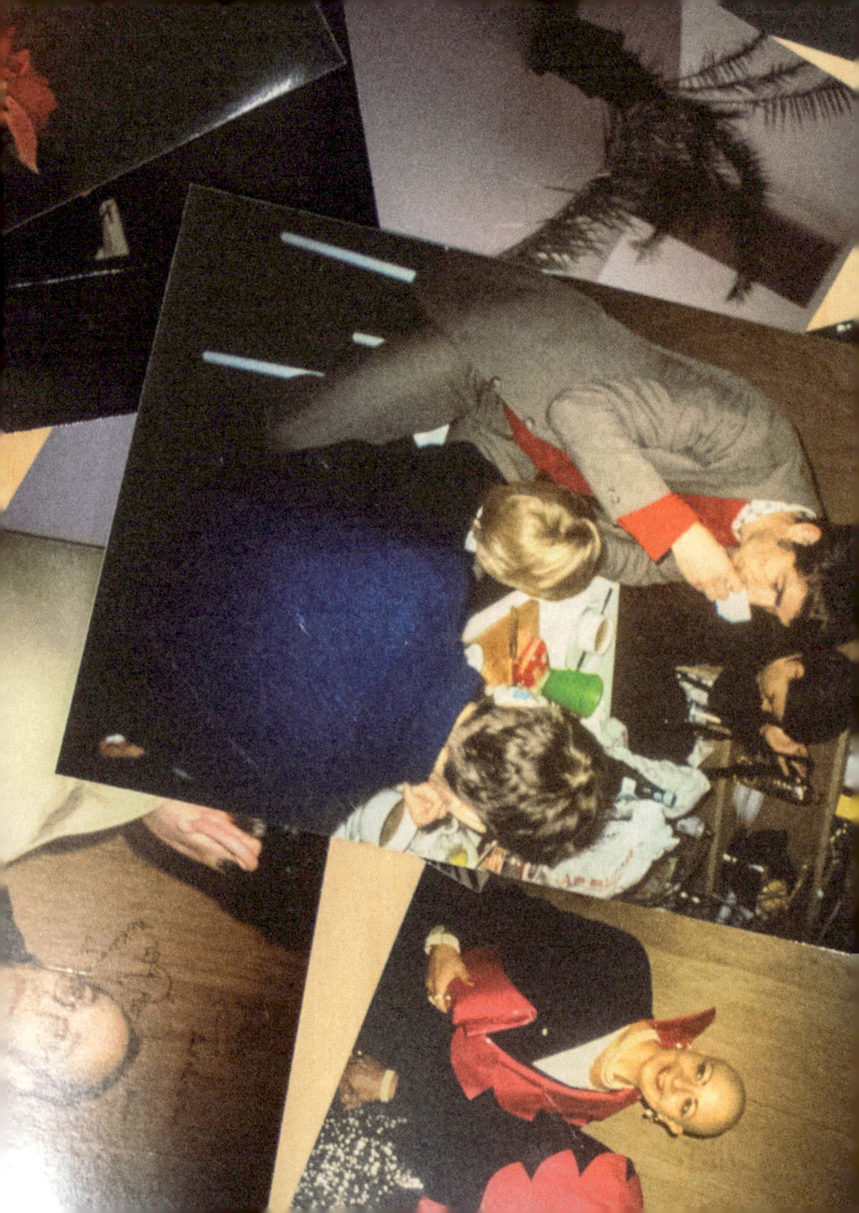

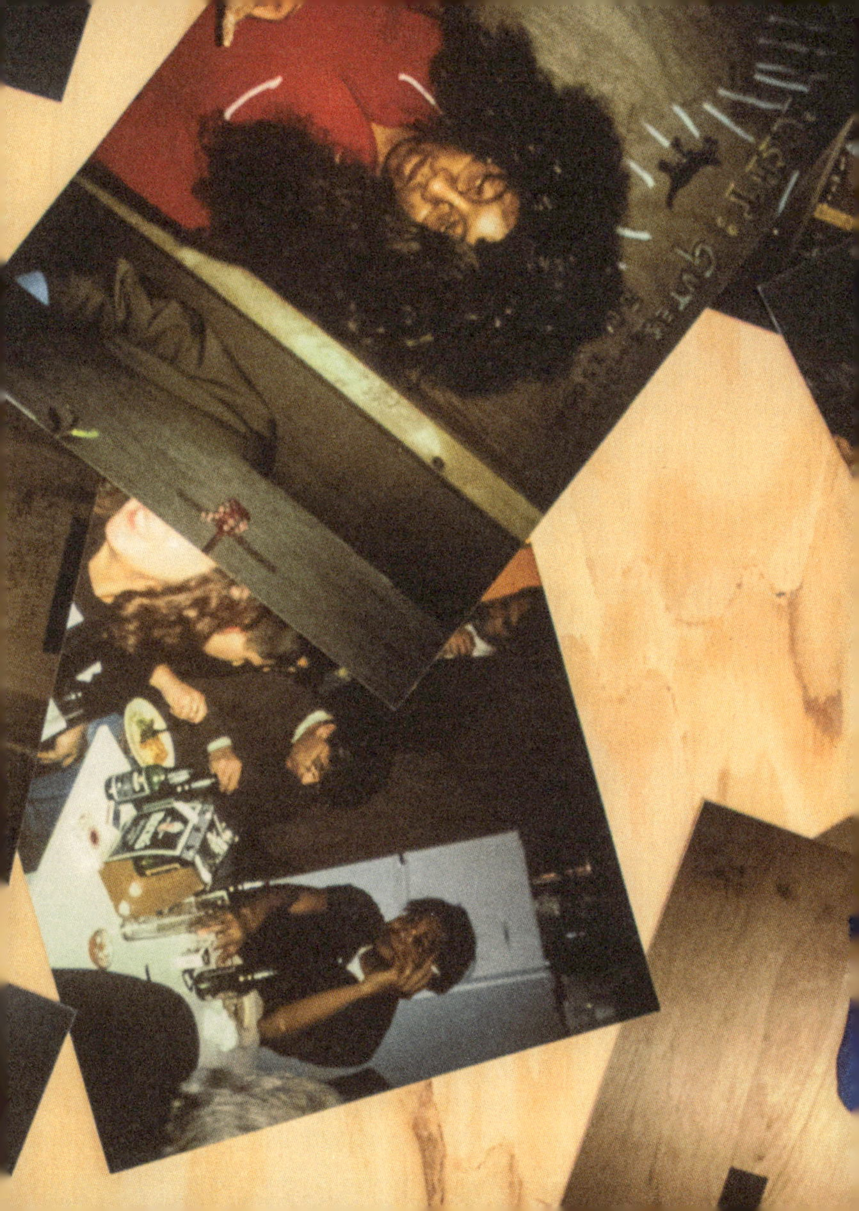

FAST RECIPE

Negroni

2 oz Monkey 47 gin
2 oz Carpano Antica Formula
sweet vermouth
2 oz Campari
1 blood orange

Slice orange into thin rounds and put aside. Combine gin, vermouth and Campari in a mixing glass over ice, add a slice of orange and stir to release the orange and cool the mixture.

Strain into a rocks glass over ice. Garnish with a fresh orange slice.

SUBMIT TO THE BLACK COMPOST

TOWARD A DO-NOTHING FARMING

Excerpt from *The One-Straw Revolution* (1975)

Masanobu Fukuoka

For thirty years I lived only in my farming and had little contact with people outside my own community. During those years I was heading in a straight line toward a "do-nothing" agricultural method.

The usual way to go about developing a method is to ask "How about trying this?" or "How about trying that?" bringing in a variety of techniques one upon the other. This is modern agriculture and it only results in making the farmer busier.

My way was opposite. I was aiming at a pleasant, natural way of farming[1] which results in making the work easier instead of harder. "How about *not* doing this? How about *not* doing that?"—that was my way of thinking. I ultimately reached the conclusion that there was no need to plow, no need to apply fertilizer, no need to make compost, no need to use insecticide. When you get

1   Farming as simply as possible within and in cooperation with the natural environment, rather than the modern approach of applying increasingly complex techniques to remake nature entirely for the benefit of human beings.

right down to it, there are few agricultural practices that are really necessary.

The reason that man's improved techniques seem to be necessary is that the natural balance has been so badly upset beforehand by those same techniques that the land has become dependent on them.

This line of reasoning not only applies to agriculture, but to other aspects of human society as well. Doctors and medicine become necessary when people create a sickly environment. Formal schooling has no intrinsic value, but becomes necessary when humanity creates a condition in which one must become "educated" to get along.

Before the end of the war, when I went up to the citrus orchard to practice what I then thought was natural farming, I did no pruning and left the orchard to itself. The branches became tangled, the trees were attacked by insects and almost two acres of mandarin orange trees withered and died.

From that time on the question, "What is the natural pattern?" was always in my mind. In the process of arriving at the answer, I wiped out another 400 trees. Finally I felt I could say with certainty: "This is the natural pattern."

To the extent that trees deviate from their natural form, pruning and insect extermination become necessary; to the extent that human society separates itself from a life close to nature, schooling becomes necessary. In nature, formal schooling has no function.

In raising children, many parents make the same mistake I made in the orchard at first. For example, teaching music to children is as unnecessary as pruning orchard trees. A child's ear catches the music. The murmuring of a stream, the sound of frogs croaking by the riverbank, the rustling of leaves in the forest, all these natural sounds are music—true music. But when a variety of disturbing noises enter and confuse the ear, the child's pure, direct appreciation of music degenerates.

If left to continue along that path, the child will be unable to hear the call of a bird or the sound of the wind as songs. That is why music education is thought to be beneficial to the child's development.

The child who is raised with an ear pure and clear may not be able to play the popular tunes on the violin or the piano, but I do not think this has anything to do with the ability to hear true music or to sing. It is when the heart is filled with song that the child can be said to be musically gifted.

Almost everyone thinks that "nature" is a good thing, but few can grasp the difference between natural and unnatural.

If a single new bud is snipped off a fruit tree with a pair of scissors, that may bring about disorder which cannot be undone. When growing according to the natural form, branches spread alternately from the trunk and the leaves receive sunlight uni-formly. If this sequence is disrupted the branches come into conflict, lie one upon another and become tangled, and the leaves wither in the places where the sun cannot penetrate. Insect damage develops. If the tree is not pruned the following year more withered branches will appear.

Human beings with their tampering do something wrong, leave the damage unrepaired, and when the adverse results accumulate, work with all their might to correct them. When the corrective actions appear to be successful, they come to view these measures as splendid accomplishments. People do this over and over again. It is as if a fool were to stomp on and break the tiles of his roof. Then when it starts to rain and the ceiling begins to rot away, he hastily climbs up to mend the damage, rejoicing in the end that he has accomplished a miraculous solution. It is the same with the scientist. He pores over books night and day, straining his eyes and becoming nearsighted, and if you wonder what on earth he has been working on all that time—it is to become the inventor of eyeglasses to correct nearsightedness.

RETURNING TO THE SOURCE

Leaning against the long handle of my scythe,
I pause in my work in the orchard and gaze out
at the mountains and the village below. I wonder
how it is that people's philosophies have come
to spin faster than the changing seasons.

The path I have followed, this natural way of farming, which strikes most people as strange, was first interpreted as a reaction against the advance and reckless development of science. But all I have been doing, farming out here in the country, is trying to show that humanity knows nothing. Because the world is moving with such furious energy in the opposite direction, it may appear that I have fallen behind the times, but I firmly believe that the path I have been following is the most sensible one.

During the past few years the number of people interested in natural farming has grown considerably. It seems that the limit of scientific development has been reached, misgivings have begun

to be felt, and the time for reappraisal has arrived.
That which was viewed as primitive and backward
is now unexpectedly seen to be far ahead of modern science. This may seem strange at first, but
I do not find it strange at all.

I discussed this with Kyoto University Professor
Iinuma recently. A thousand years ago agriculture
was practiced in Japan without plowing, and it
was not until the Tokugawa Era 300–400 years
ago that shallow cultivation was introduced. Deep
plowing came to Japan with Western agriculture.
I said that in coping with the problems of the
future the next generation would return to the
non-cultivation method.

To grow crops in an unplowed field may seem at
first a regression to primitive agriculture, but over
the years this method has been shown in university
laboratories and agricultural testing centers across
the country to be the most simple, efficient, and
up-to-date method of all. Although this way of
farming disavows modern science, it now has come

to stand in the forefront of modern agricultural development.

I presented this "direct seeding non-cultivation winter grain/rice succession" in agricultural journals twenty years ago. From then on it appeared often in print and was introduced to the public at large on radio and television programs many times, but nobody paid much attention to it.

Now suddenly, it is a completely different story. You might say that natural farming has become the rage. Journalists, professors, and technical researchers are flocking to visit my fields and the huts up on the mountain.

Different people see it from different points of view, make their own interpretations, and then leave. One sees it as primitive, another as back-ward, someone else considers it the pinnacle of agricultural achievement, and a fourth hails it as a breakthrough into the future. In general, people are only concerned with whether this kind of farming is an advance into the future or a revival of times past. Few are able to grasp correctly that natural farming arises from the unmoving and unchanging center of agricultural development.

To the extent that people separate themselves from nature, they spin out further and further from the center. At the same time, a centripetal effect asserts itself and the desire to return to nature arises. But if people merely become caught up in reacting, moving to the left or to the right, depending on conditions, the result is only more activity. The non-moving point of origin, which lies outside the realm of relativity, is passed over, unnoticed. I believe that even "returning-to-nature" and anti-pollution activities, no matter how commendable, are not moving toward a genuine solution if they are carried out solely in reaction to the overdevelopment of the present age.

Nature does not change, although the way of viewing nature invariably changes from age to age.

No matter the age, natural farming exists forever
as the wellspring of agriculture.

ONE REASON THAT NATURAL FARMING HAS NOT SPREAD

Over the past twenty or thirty years this method
of growing rice and winter grain has been
tested over a wide range of climates and natural
conditions. Almost every prefecture in Japan
has run tests comparing yields of "direct seeding
non-cultivation" with those of paddy rice growing
and the usual ridge and furrow rye and barley
cultivation. These tests have produced no evidence
to contradict the universal applicability of natural
farming.

And so one may ask why this truth has not spread.
I think that one of the reasons is that the world
has become so specialized that it has become impossible for people to grasp anything in its entirety.
For example, an expert in insect damage prevention

from the Kochi Prefectural Testing Center came to inquire why there were so few rice leaf-hoppers in my fields even though I had not used insecticide. Upon investigating the habitat, the balance between insects and their natural enemies, the rate of spider propagation and so on, the leaf-hoppers were found to be just as scarce in my fields as in the Center's fields, which are sprayed countless times with a variety of deadly chemicals.

The professor was also surprised to find that while the harmful insects were few, their natural predators were far more numerous in my fields than in the sprayed fields. Then it dawned on him that the fields were being maintained in this state by means of a natural balance established among the various insect communities. He acknowledged that if my method were generally adopted, the problem of crop devastation by leaf-hoppers could be solved. He then got into his car and returned to Kochi.

But if you ask whether or not the testing center's soil fertility or crop specialists have come here,

the answer is no, they have not. And if you were
to suggest at a conference or gathering that this
method, or rather non-method, be tried on a
wide scale, it is my guess that the prefecture or
research station would reply, "Sorry, it's too early
for that. We must first carry out research from
every possible angle before giving final approval."
It would take years for a conclusion to come down.

This sort of thing goes on all the time. Specialists
and technicians from all over Japan have come
to this farm. Seeing the fields from the standpoint
of his own specialty, every one of these researchers
has found them at least satisfactory, if not remark-
able. But in the five or six years since the professor
from the research station came to visit here,
there have been few changes in Kochi Prefecture.

This year the agricultural department of Kinki
University has set up a natural farming project
team in which students of several different depart-
ments will come here to conduct investigations.
This approach may be one step nearer, but I have

a feeling that the next move may be two steps in the opposite direction.

Self-styled experts often comment, "The basic idea of the method is all right, but wouldn't it be more convenient to harvest by machine?" or, "Wouldn't the yield be greater if you used fertilizer or pesticide in certain cases or at certain times?" There are always those who try to mix natural and scientific farming. But this way of thinking completely misses the point. The farmer who moves toward compromise can no longer criticize science at the fundamental level.

Natural farming is gentle and easy and indicates a return to the source of farming. A single step away from the source can only lead one astray.

HUMANITY DOES NOT KNOW NATURE

Lately I have been thinking that the point must
be reached when scientists, politicians, artists,
philosophers, men of religion, and all those who
work in the fields should gather here, gaze out
over these fields, and talk things over together.
I think this is the kind of thing that must happen
if people are to see beyond their specialties.

Scientists think they can understand nature.
That is the stand they take. Because they are
convinced that they can understand nature, they
are committed to investigating nature and putting
it to use. But I think an understanding of nature
lies beyond the reach of human intelligence.

I often tell the young people in the huts on the
mountain, who come here to help out and to
learn about natural farming, that anybody can
see the trees up on the mountain. They can see
the green of the leaves; they can see the rice plants.
They think they know what green is. In contact

with nature morning and night, they sometimes come to think that they know nature. But when they think they are beginning to understand nature, they can be sure that they are on the wrong track.

Why is it impossible to know nature? That which is conceived to be nature is only the *idea* of nature arising in each person's mind. The ones who see true nature are infants. They see without thinking, straight and clear. If even the names of plants are known, a mandarin orange tree of the citrus family, a pine of the pine family, nature is not seen in its true form.

An object seen in isolation from the whole is not the real thing.

Specialists in various fields gather together and observe a stalk of rice. The insect disease specialist sees only insect damage, the specialist in plant nutrition considers only the plant's vigor. This is unavoidable as things are now.

As an example, I told the gentleman from the research station when he was investigating the relation between rice leaf-hoppers and spiders in my fields, "Professor, since you are researching spiders, you are interested in only one among the many natural predators of the leaf-hopper. This year spiders appeared in great numbers, but last year it was toads. Before that, it was frogs that predominated. There are countless variations."

It is impossible for specialized research to grasp the role of a single predator at a certain time within the intricacy of insect inter-relationships. There are seasons when the leaf-hopper population is low because there are many spiders. There are times when a lot of rain falls and frogs cause the spiders to disappear, or when little rain falls and neither leaf-hoppers nor frogs appear at all.

Methods of insect control which ignore the relationships among the insects themselves are truly useless. Research on spiders and leaf-hoppers must also consider the relation between frogs and spiders.

When things have reached this point, a frog professor will also be needed. Experts on spiders and leaf-hoppers, another on rice, and another expert on water management will all have to join the gathering.

Furthermore, there are four or five different kinds of spiders in these fields. I remember a few years ago when somebody came rushing over to the house early one morning to ask me if I had covered my fields with a silk net or something. I could not imagine what he was talking about, so I hurried straight out to take a look.

We had just finished harvesting the rice, and overnight the rice stubble and low-lying grasses had become completely covered with spider webs, as though with silk. Waving and sparkling with the morning mist, it was a magnificent sight.

The wonder of it is that when this happens, as it does only once in a great while, it only lasts for a day or two. If you look closely there are several spiders in every square inch. They are so thick on the field that there is hardly any space between them. In a quarter acre there must be how many thousands, how many millions! When you go to look at the field two or three days later, you see that strands of web several yards long have broken off and are waving about in the wind with five or six spiders clinging to each one. It is like when dandelion fluff or pine cone seeds are blown away in the wind. The young spiders cling to the strands and are sent sailing off in the sky.

The spectacle is an amazing natural drama. Seeing this, you understand that poets and artists will also have to join in the gathering.

When chemicals are put into a field, this is all destroyed in an instant. I once thought there would be nothing wrong with putting ashes from the fireplace onto the fields.[2] The result was astounding.

2   Mr. Fukuoka makes compost of his wood ashes and other organic household wastes. He applies this to his small kitchen garden.

Two or three days later the field was completely bare of spiders. The ashes had caused the strands of web to disintegrate. How many thousands of spiders fell victim to a single handful of this apparently harmless ash? Applying an insecticide is not simply a matter of eliminating the leaf-hoppers together with their natural predators. Many other essential dramas of nature are affected.

The phenomenon of these great swarms of spiders, which appear in the rice fields in the autumn and like escape artists vanish overnight, is still not understood. No one knows where they come from, how they survive the winter, or where they go when they disappear.

And so the use of chemicals is not a problem for the entomologist alone. Philosophers, men of religion, artists and poets must also help to decide whether or not it is permissible to use chemicals in farming, and what the results of using even organic fertilizers might be.

We will harvest about 22 bushels (1,300 pounds) of rice, and 22 bushels of winter grain from each quarter acre of this land. If the harvest reaches 29 bushels, as it sometimes does, you might not be able to find a greater harvest if you searched the whole country. Since advanced technology had nothing to do with growing this grain, it stands as a contradiction to the assumptions of modern science. Anyone who will come and see these fields and accept their testimony, will feel deep misgivings over the question of whether or not humans know nature, and of whether or not nature can be known within the confines of human understanding.

The irony is that science has served only to show how small human knowledge is.

Masanobu Fukuoka, *The One-Straw Revolution*, published by New York Review Books, 2009, pp. 15–32. Reprinted with the kind permission of Michiyo Shibuya, The Fukuoka Estate.

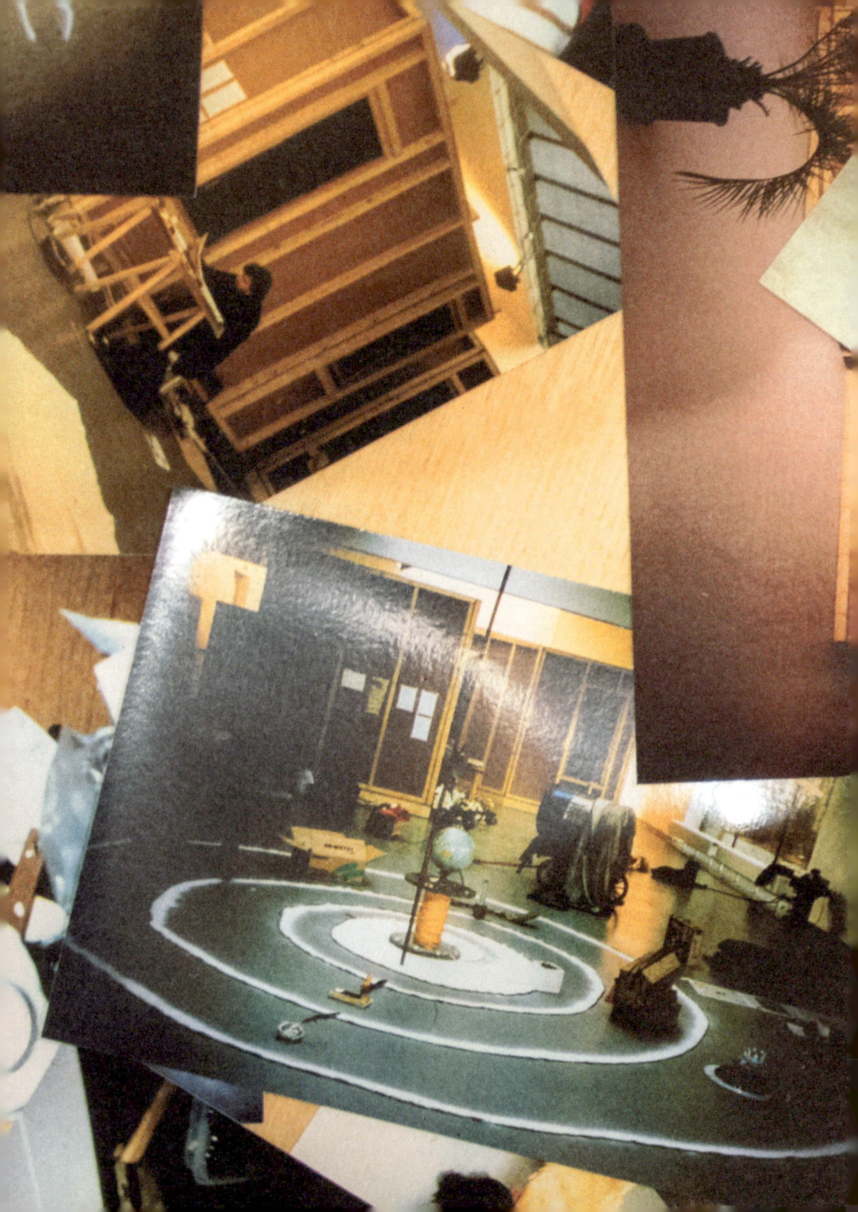

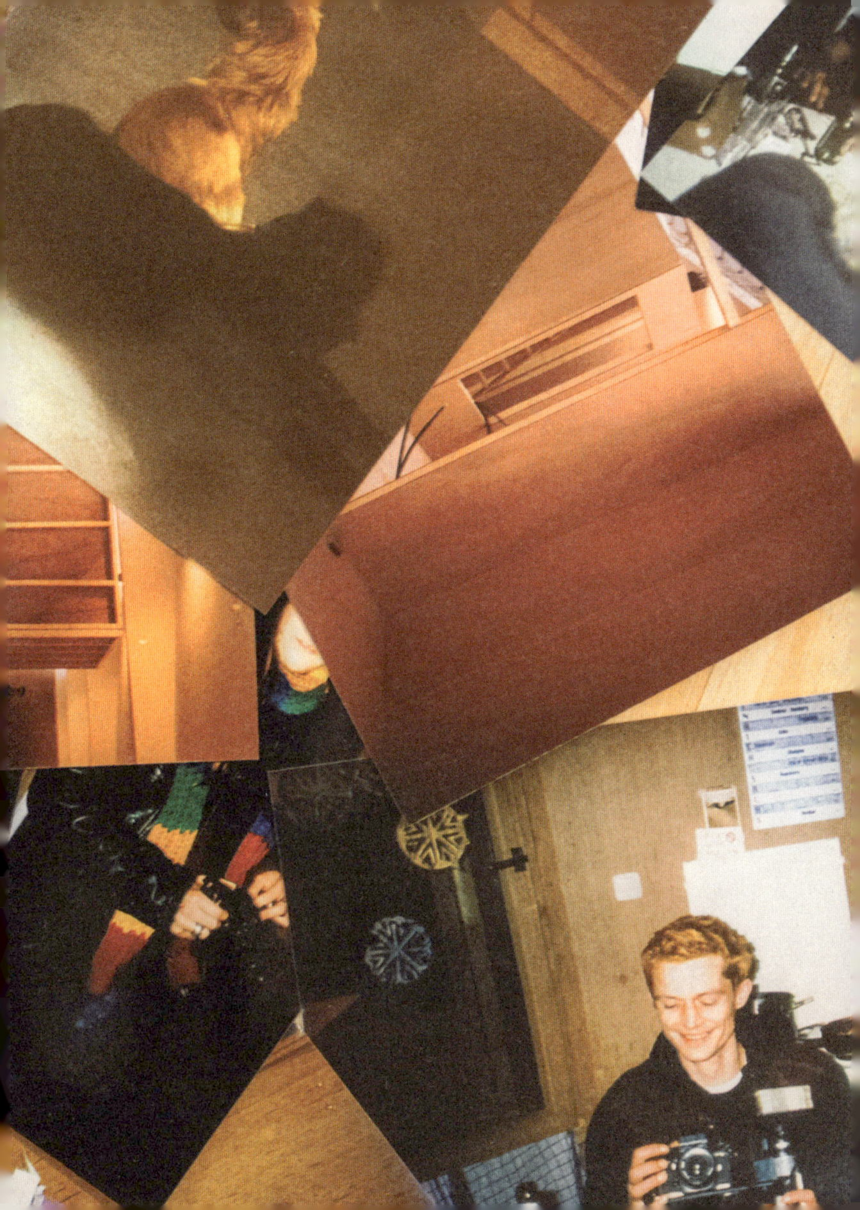

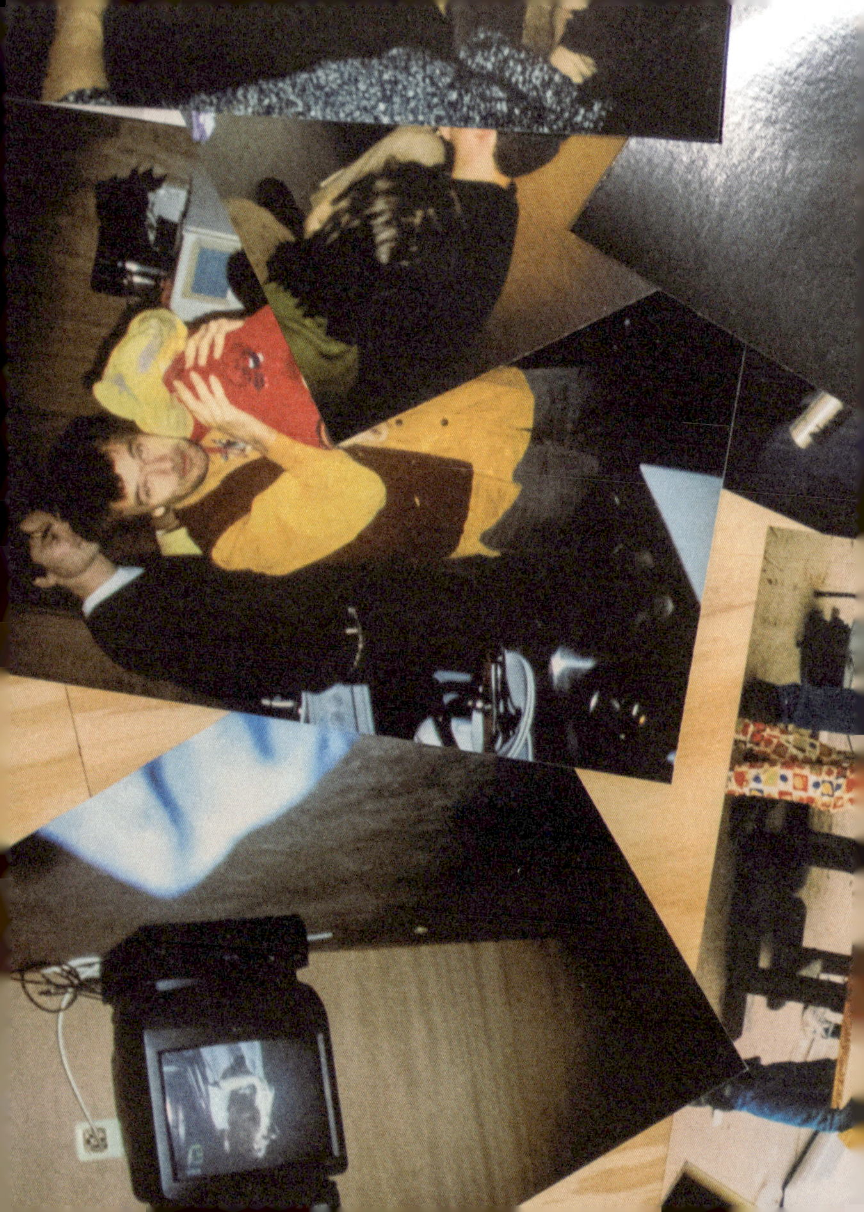

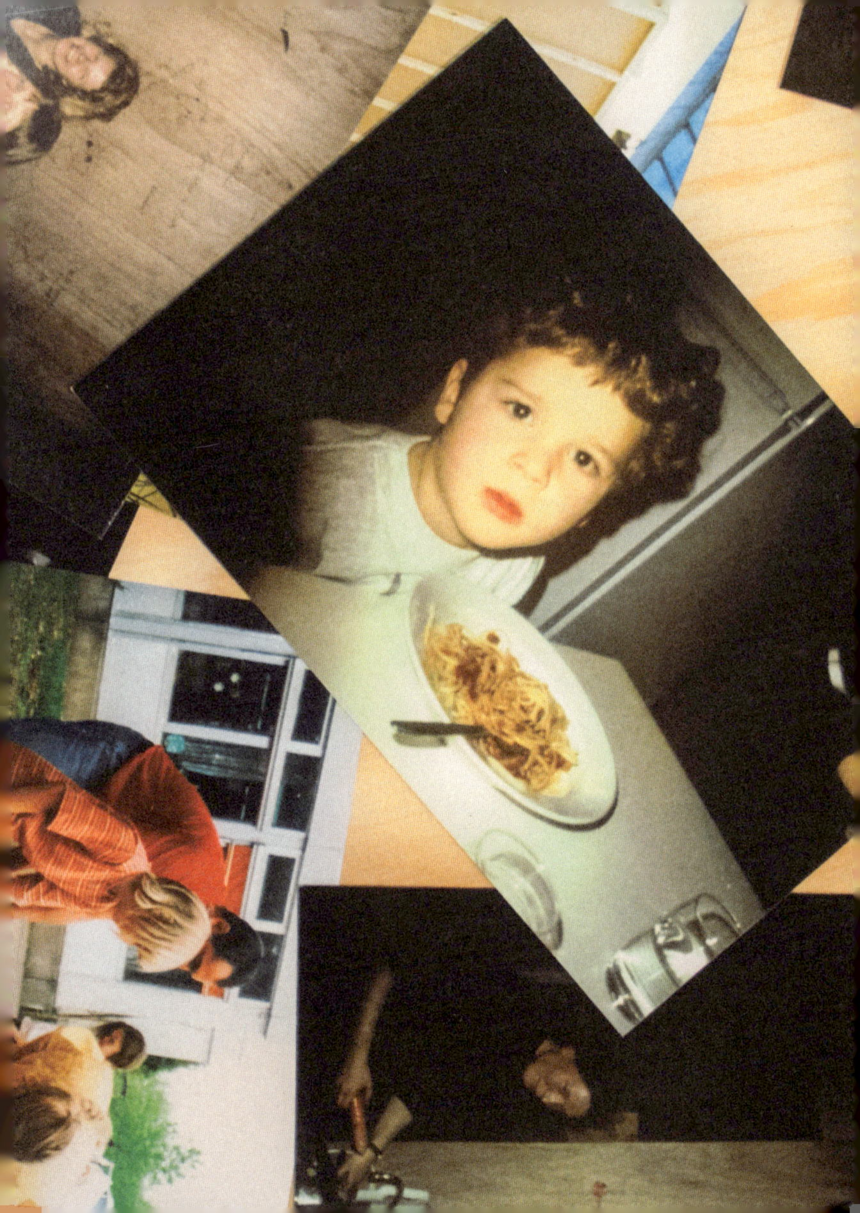

HOW TO MAKE COMPOST

Add Green Material

Green material is high in nitrogen. It includes kitchen scraps such as coffee grounds, peelings, fruit cores, uneaten leftovers and eggshells. Any kitchen waste that is not greasy, dairy or meat can be composted. Grass clippings, leaves and weeds are also considered green materials, as is manure from barnyard animals (herbivores such as cattle or horses, but not cats or dogs).

Add Brown Material

Brown material is high in carbon. Paper, cornstalks, sawdust, small branches, twigs and straw all fall into this category.

The ratio of nitrogen to carbon should ideally be 50/50 in your compost pile so for every bit of brown material you add, be sure to balance it with green material.

Tip

If you add paper, such as newspaper, to your compost pile, shred it first so that oxygen can get at a significant amount of the surface. If you don't take this step, you risk it turning moldy and ruining your compost.

Add Water

Water is the final key ingredient in a thriving compost pile. Without moisture, your pile will take months to do anything and, if dry enough, will not break down at all. If your pile is too wet, on the other hand, it will smell and become slimy as the ratio of harmful bacteria outweighs the good. You want the pile to remain damp but not dripping wet. If you do not get enough rainfall to suffice, dump a bucket of water over it once a week to keep things moving. You will know that your compost pile is right if it becomes hot in the middle. Maintaining heat is important to sterilise the compost and kill the weed seeds or harmful bacteria that may be there. The heat is your proof that the ratio is working for your compost pile.

Turn the Pile Regularly

Whether using a compost bin or a simple pile, you will need to turn your materials with a shovel or pitchfork. Simply move the outer portion of the pile toward the center, turning each scoop over as you go.

Continue shuffling the materials until you have exposed the decomposing materials within the pile.

A compost pile needs to be turned every two to four weeks. If you have a bin with a crank, give it a few turns every week.

If your pile heats up, is adequately moist and gets turned regularly, you should have usable compost in one to two months.

Harvest the Compost

When most of the contents have broken down (this will happen to the bottom layer first), the compost is mature and ready to harvest. Tilt or wiggle the bin to loosen the compost and shovel out the compost that's ready, formed and

broken down fully. Turn the remaining
compost and allow it to continue to
break down.

Use the Harvested Compost

Harvested compost can be used in many
ways. In addition to working it into garden
beds, you can also use it as mulch or
add it to potting soil. If using it in garden
beds, you can sprinkle it on top of the soil
or rake it into the soil.

How to Use Your Compost

Fertiliser: Feed your perennials, bulbs,
fruit trees, container plants or lawn.
Top dress or sprinkle some on top
of your new or established plantings.

Mulch: Apply a 3- to 6-inch layer of compost to the soil surface instead of using mulch, it will prevent water evaporation from the soil, keeping it moist longer, and it will also discourage weed growth.

Potting soil: To make an enriched potting soil, use equal parts compost, vermiculite and topsoil, mix thoroughly.

Compost tea: Brew compost tea. By making a liquid emulsion, you get a concentrated fertiliser that quickly reaches your plant's roots.

HAPPINESS IS NOT ALWAYS FUN

SLOW RECIPE

Dedduang's Fish Sauce

Two parts salt
Three parts fresh caught anchovies
Pineapple
Dried onion and garlic stalks
Sugar

Combine all the ingredients except for
the sugar, mix and transfer to a large clay
jar. Cover with more salt. Cover the vat
with a loosely fitted lid to allow for air
to circulate. Leave to ferment for at least
twelve months. After one year of fermenta-
tion, slowly drain the vat. This process can
take up to one week, do not rush it.

Transfer the resulting liquid into a large
drum over an open fire and bring to a boil.

Once it reaches its boiling point, add the
sugar and briefly simmer until dissolved.
Ladle off the sauce into a separate vat
for cooling and leave exposed to open
air and sunlight for several days to finish.

Bottle and Enjoy.

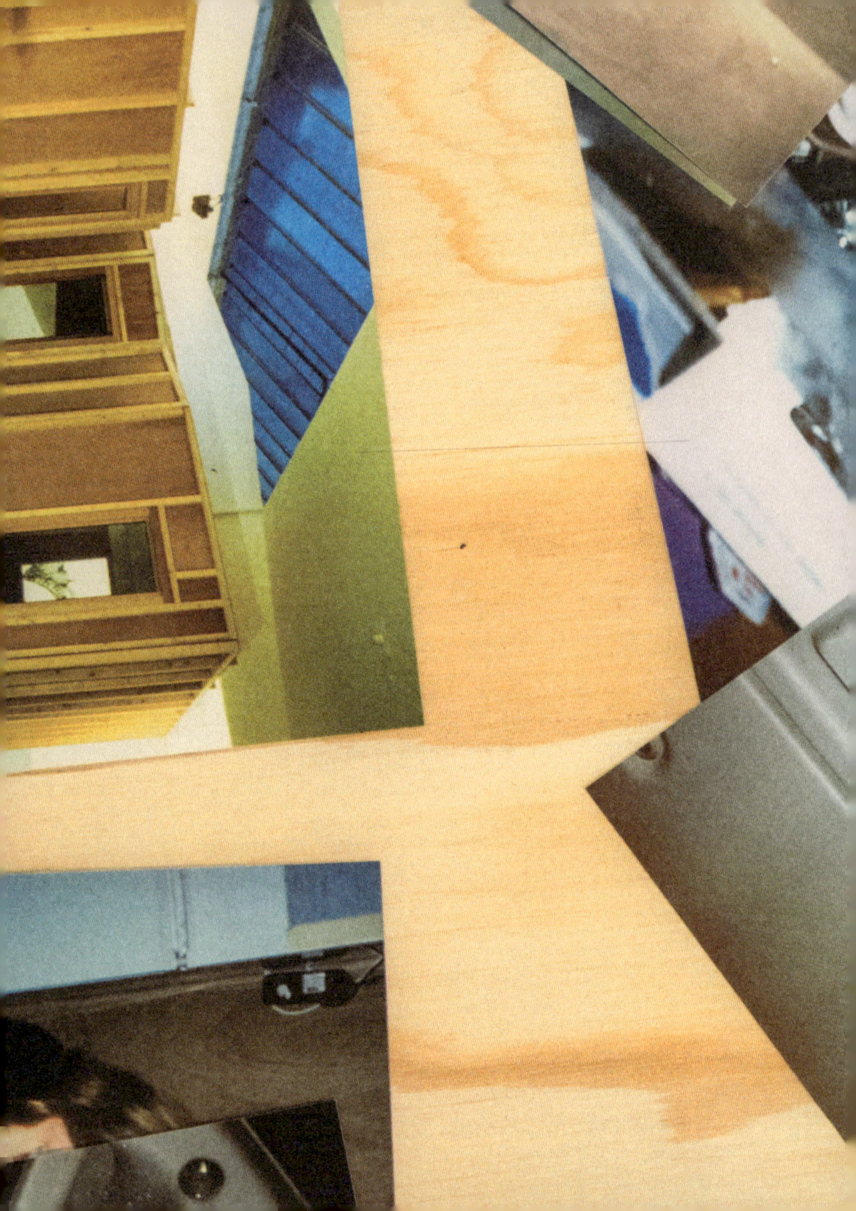

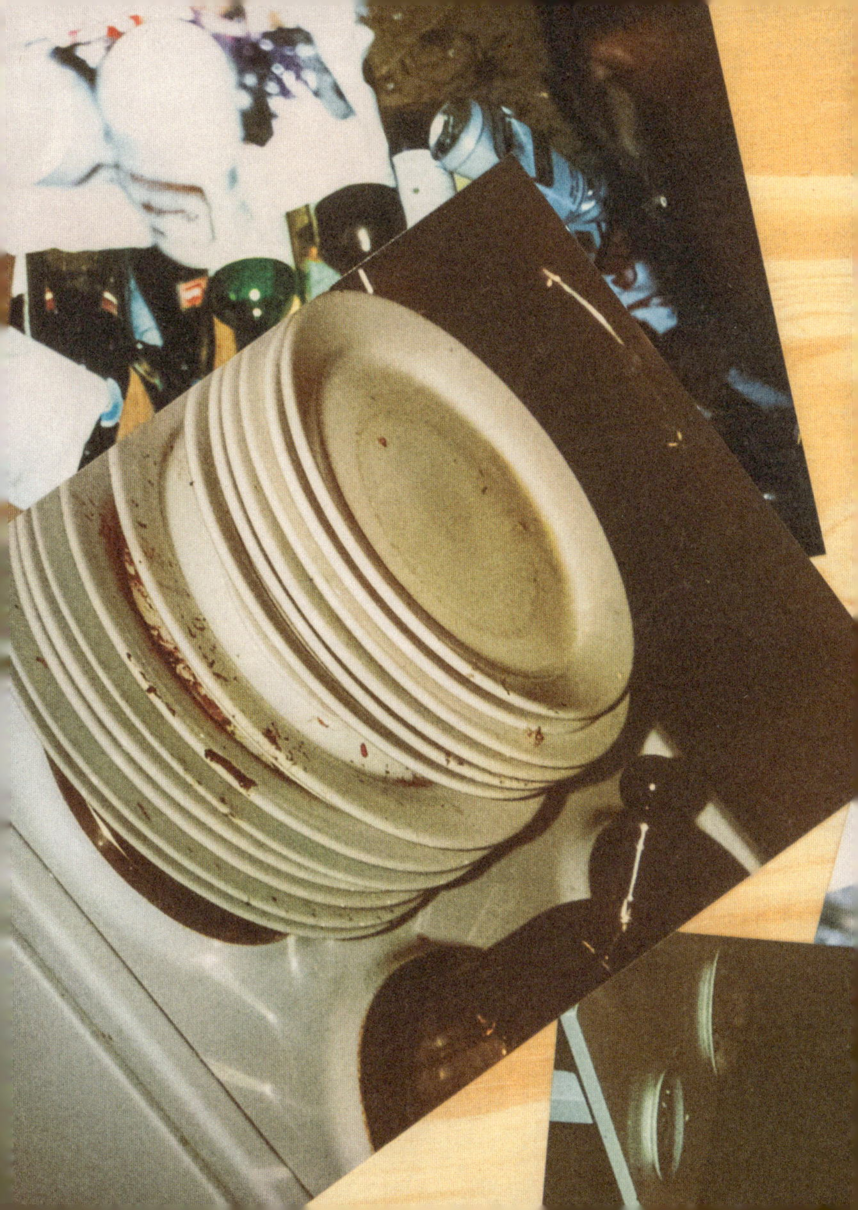

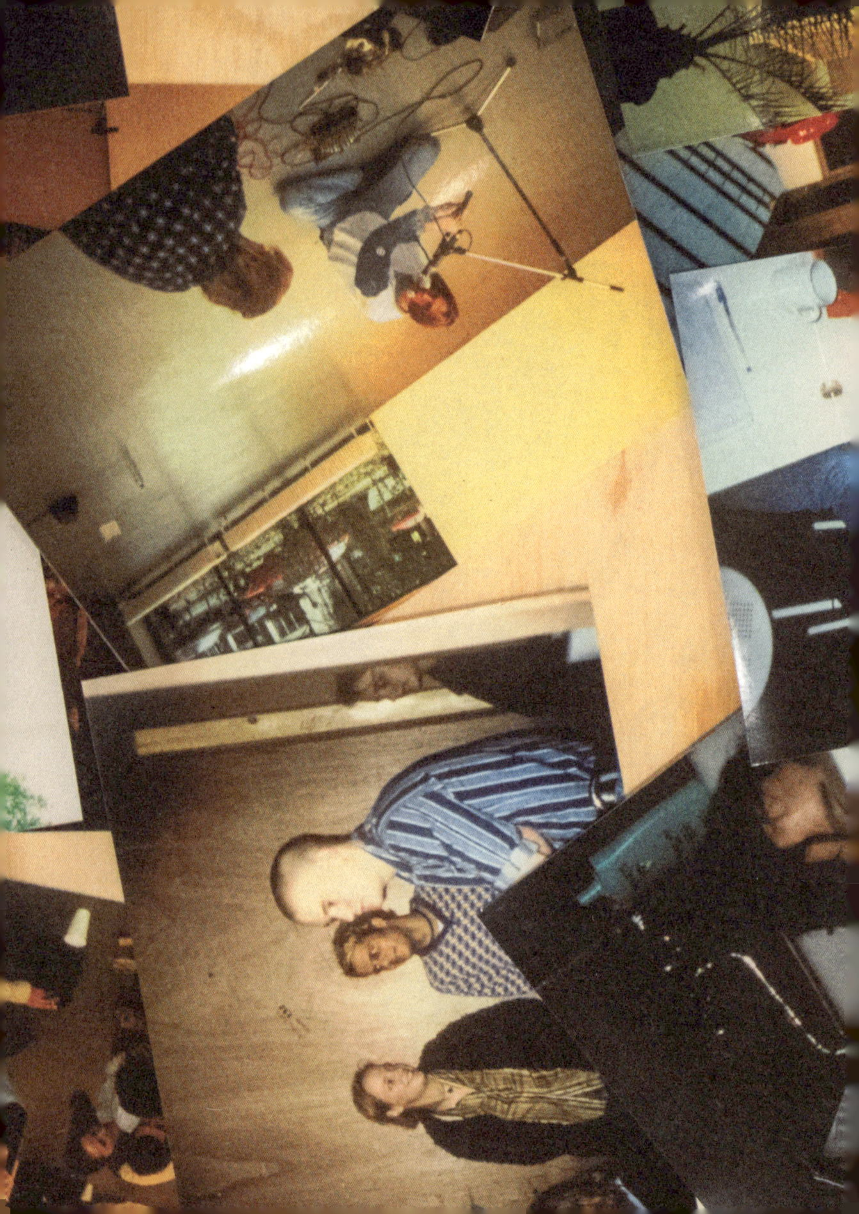

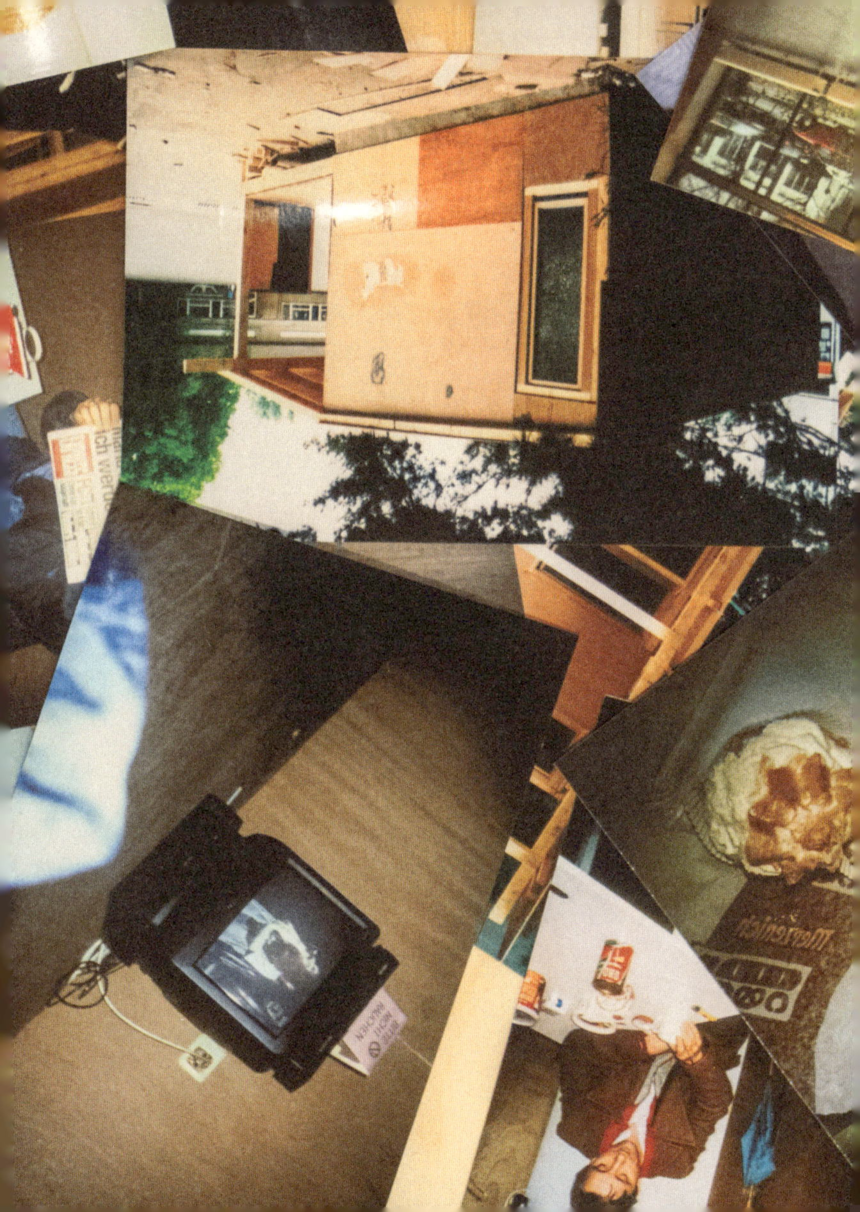

THE
DAYS
OF
THIS
SOCIETY
IS
NUMBERED

APPENDIX

Biographies

Rirkrit Tiravanija (born 1961 in Buenos Aires) is an artist working across multiple disciplines. Introducing communal activities such as conversation, music and games, drinking and cooking into exhibitions, Tiravanija gained international recognition. By transforming art into social situations, he explicitly formulated a critique, questioning stereotypical portrayals of Asian cultures and racist clichés within Western contexts. He grew up in a Thai diplomatic family, living in various cities including Buenos Aires, Bangkok, Addis Ababa and Toronto, before enrolling at the Ontario College of Art in Ottawa, Canada, to study photo journalism. In 1984, he moved to the United States to study at the School of the Art Institute of Chicago and later at the Whitney Museum of American Art Independent Study Program (ISP) in New York. He made his first installations in the mid-1980s.

With the exhibition *DAS GLÜCK IST NICHT IMMER LUSTIG* (Happiness is not always fun) (12.9.2024–12.1.2025) Gropius Bau presents more than 80 of the artist's works created between 1987 and 2024. The exhibition takes its title from the opening sequence of Rainer Werner Fassbinder's film *Ali: Fear Eats the Soul* (1974), an important point of reference for Tiravanija. Living and working in New York, Chiang Mai and Berlin, Tiravanija has repeatedly referred to cultural clichés and politics in Germany since the early 1990s.

Masanobu Fukuoka (1913–2008) was born and raised on the Japanese island of Shikoku. He was the son of a rice farmer who was also the local mayor. Fukuoka studied plant pathology and worked as a produce inspector in Yokohama. In 1938 he returned to his village home determined to put his ideas about natural farming into practice. During World War II, he worked for the Japanese government as a researcher on food production, managing to avoid military service until the final few months of the war. After the war, he devoted himself wholeheartedly to farming. In 1975, distressed by the effects of Japan's post-war modernisation, Fukuoka wrote *The One-Straw Revolution*. In his later years, Fukuoka was involved in several projects to reduce desertification. He remained an active farmer until well into his eighties, and continued to give lectures until only a few years before his death at the age of ninety-five. Fukuoka is also the author of *The Natural Way of Farming* and *The Road Back to Nature*.

References

Notes for *untitled 1992 (free)* → p. 17

Photocopy
Courtesy of the artist

For *untitled 1992 (free)*, his first solo exhibition with 303 Gallery in New York City in 1992, Tiravanija relocated all movable content (storage, kitchen, bathroom, office) of the gallery to the exhibition space. All doors inside the gallery were unhinged and displayed leaning against the walls of the office in the back of the gallery where a curry kitchen had been set up. On two gas cookers the artist or friends frequently cooked lunch for visitors during the exhibition: one spicy curry with Thai ingredients, and a milder, westernised version with some ingredients replaced by local substitutes. For this publication we are reproducing Tiravanija's personal notes written in preparation for the exhibition in 1992.

Detail of *untitled 1996
(tomorrow is another day)*, 1996

Courtesy of the artist
Image: © Gropius Bau

→ pp. 8–11,
20–23, 50–53,
80–83, 98–101,
118–121

For *untitled 1996 (tomorrow is another day)*,
his solo show at the Kölnischer Kunstverein in
1996, Tiravanija produced a 1:1 plywood replica
of his NYC apartment. The structure was fully
functional, equipped with bathroom and cooking
facilities. Throughout the exhibition, the structure
and the whole exhibition space were open to the
public 24 hours per day, except on Sundays when
the Kunstverein was closed due to labour regu-
lations. Both the apartment and the surrounding
space were heavily used by visitors, for parties,
a wedding, concerts, exhibitions, dinners, people
spending the night, taking baths, etc.

A Different Kind of Nothing → p. 15

Submit to the Black Compost → p. 57

This appeal is the last line of a poem by Édouard Glissant from his 1969 book *Poetic Intention*.

Happiness is Not Always Fun → p. 93

This quote is taken from Rainer Werner Fassbinder's film *Ali: Fear Eats the Soul* (1974), an important point of reference for Rirkrit Tiravanija.

The Days of This Society Is Numbered → p. 103

This statement by Guy Debord, co-founder of the Avantgarde movement Situationist International, is intentionally mistranslated by Rirkrit Tiravanija.

Gropius Bau

Located in the centre of Berlin, the Gropius Bau is a lively place to encounter art and each other. The internationally renowned institution stages large-scale exhibitions and performances by contemporary artists. Its diverse events focus on exchange and discussion, bringing together local and global perspectives.

Here, artists shape the programme from within, not only showing their own work, but developing thematic or solo exhibitions of work by other artists. In some cases, they spend several years working in one of the Gropius Bau's on-site studios, becoming deeply intertwined with the institution and shaping it with their ideas and vision.

In all of this, the notion of playing serves as a proposition for how we can engage with one another in times of increasing social tension: openly rather than judgmentally, with each other rather

than against each other and playfully exchang-
ing perspectives and positions. This idea also
lies at the heart of BAUBAU, a play space for
kids developed by artist Kerstin Brätsch and
accessible free of charge. Here, kids are invited
to take up space, make noise, let off steam
and constantly reinvent a space where more
is allowed than forbidden.

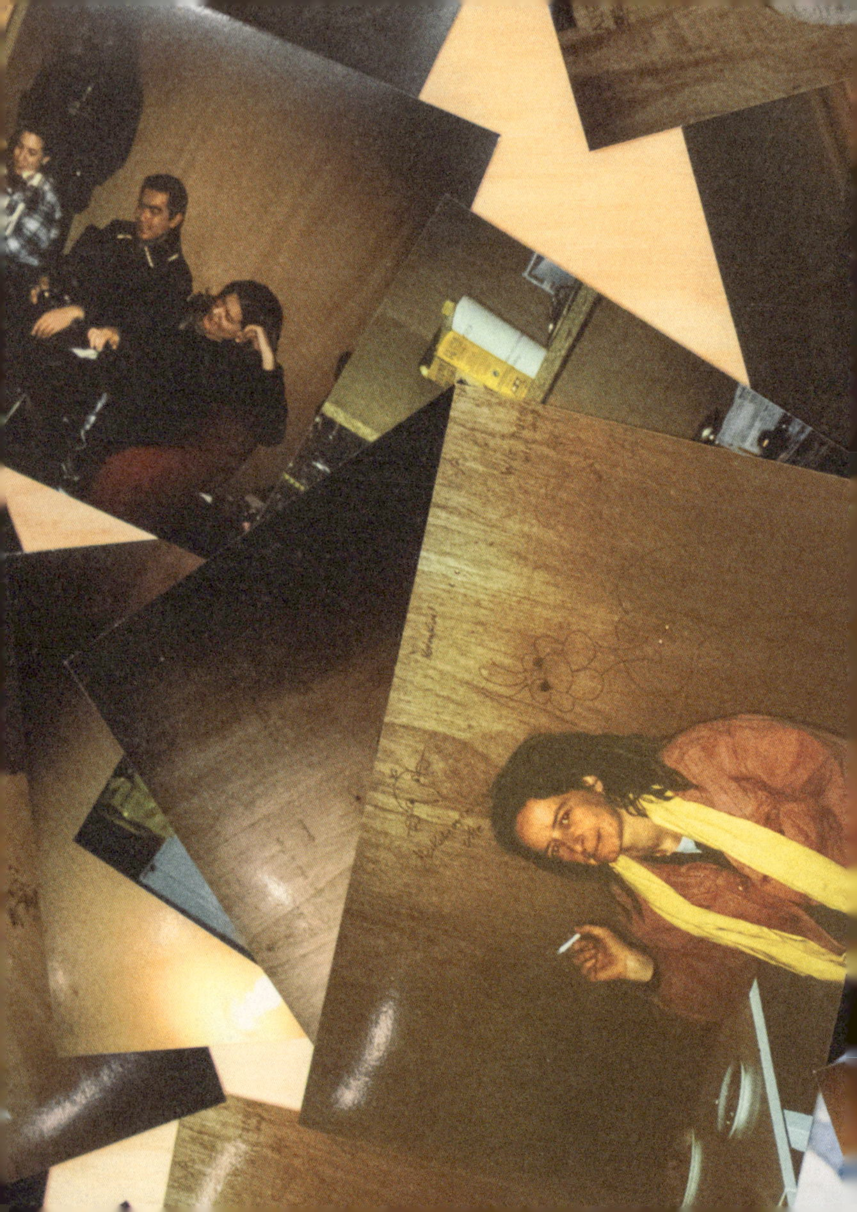

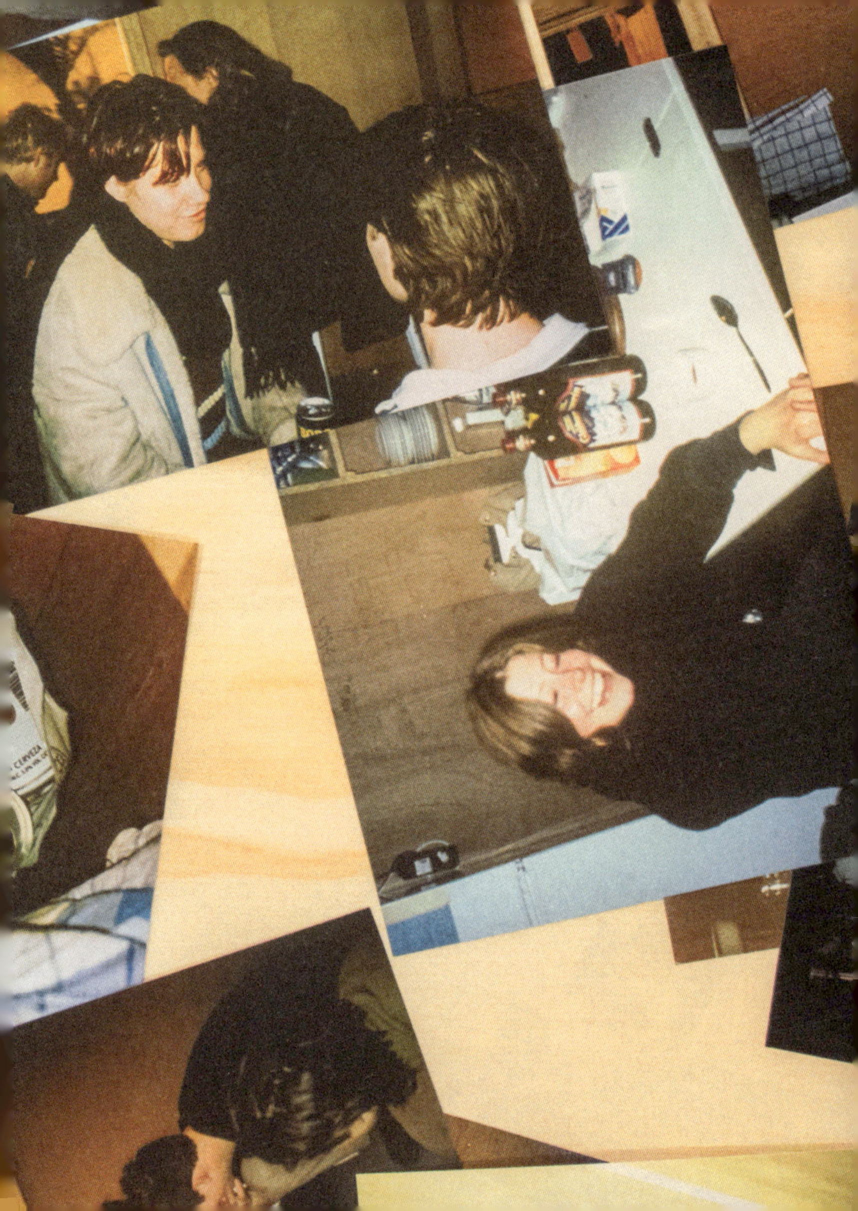

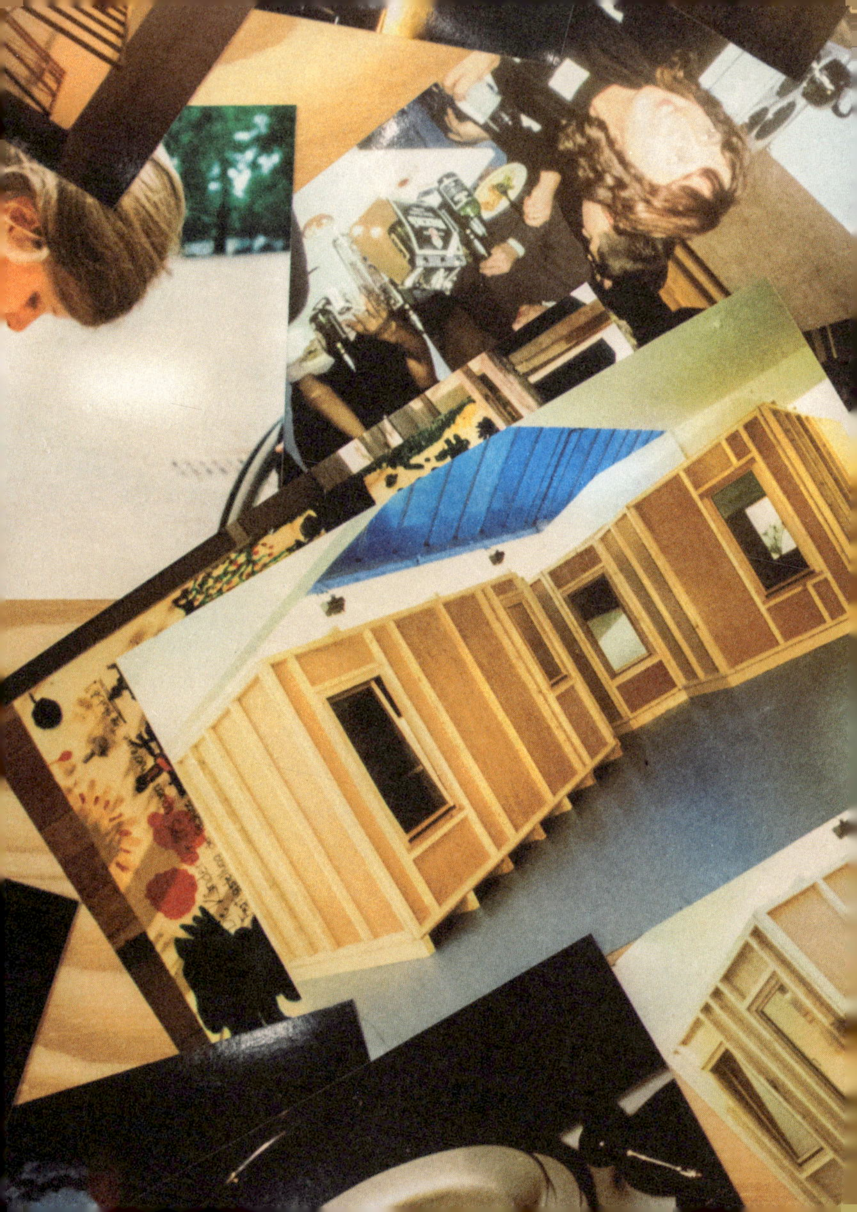

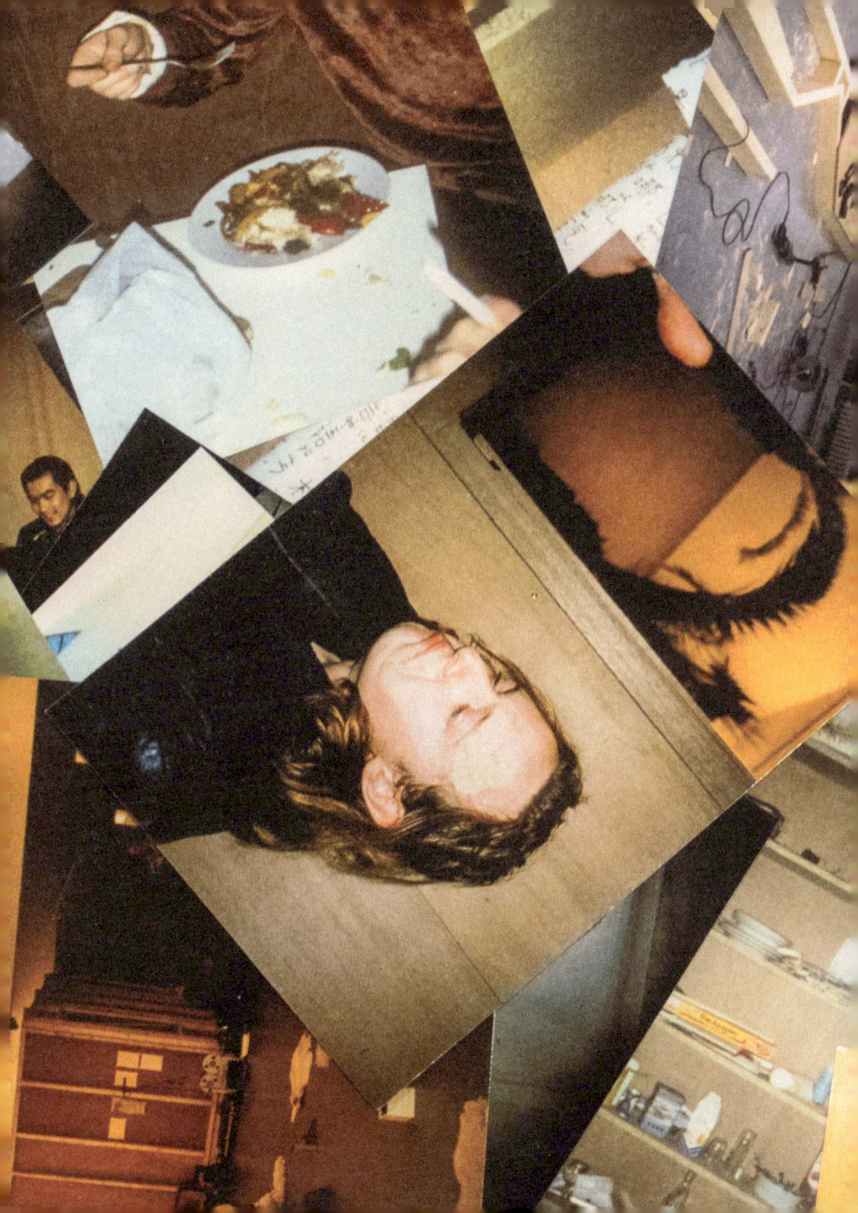

Afterword by the German
Federal Cultural Foundation

"Take the pot out of the museum display case and cook in it." Rirkrit Tiravanija sees artworks as social spaces that enable people to meet, interact and share experiences. The exhibition at Gropius Bau showed the range of his works, which are always experiments as well. That the new Gropius Bau publication series begins with Rirkrit Tiravanija is therefore fitting. The series is also daring: It assembles artists' books giving carte blanche, or – to stay in the image of the exhibition – a "white cube," allowing artists to design exactly 128 pages as they please. These unusual publications provide insights into artistic thinking and subjects in a more playful and accessible way. We congratulate the Gropius Bau and the artist on the impressive exhibition and the first volume of the new publication series *The Practice – What Moves Artists*, edited by Jenny Schlenzka and Julia Grosse. We hope it finds many

inspired readers and wish them great pleasure
with Rirkrit Tiravanija's reflections on the beauties
and difficulties of making less and doing nothing
as a practice.

Katarzyna Wielga-Skolimowska
Executive Board / Artistic Director

Kirsten Haß
Executive Board / Administrative Director

Imprint

Rirkrit Tiravanija,
On Making Less is published
as volume 1 of the book series
The Practice—What Moves Artists,
accompanying the exhibition
RIRKRIT TIRAVANIJA:
HAPPINESS IS
NOT ALWAYS FUN
12 September 2024–
12 January 2025
at Gropius Bau, Berlin.

© 2024 The editors, author
and artist and Bierke Verlag

Editors and Concept:
Jenny Schlenzka & Julia Grosse
Project Lead: Kirsten Einfeldt
Editorial Team:
Julia Grosse, Jan Pfeiffer,
Christopher Wierling
Image Editing: Julia Grosse,
Luis Kürschner,
Christopher Wierling
Rights: Savannah Thümler
Translations (German–
English): Faith Ann Gibson
Translations (English–
German): Tobias Haberkorn
Copy-editing (English):
Faith Ann Gibson
Copy-editing (German):
Claudius Prößer

Graphic Design:
Stoodio Santiago da Silva
Typefaces: Helvetica, Arial,
Futura, Garamond, Times
New Roman, New Century
Schoolbook, Andale Mono
Paper: Arena Rough,
Munken Print White
Printing and Image
Processing: Mundschenk
Druck + Medien,
Lutherstadt Wittenberg

Berliner Festspiele/
Gropius Bau
A division of
Kulturveranstaltungen
des Bundes in Berlin
(KBB) GmbH:

Matthias Pees: Director
Charlotte Sieben:
Managing Director

Director's Office

Cordula Brucker:
Assistant to the Director
Kirsten Einfeldt: Institutional
Funding & Publications
Julia Grosse:
Strategic Consulting and
Conceptual Development
Lusine Khurshudyan:
Student Assistant
Wiebke Koch: Organisation
& Strategic Partnerships
Carlos Rodriguez Artavia:
Financial & Administrative
Organisation
Ana Rodriguez Schlittgen:
Student Assistant
Jenny Schlenzka: Director
Savannah Thümler:
Fellow to the Director

Curatorial Team

Nora-Swantje Almes:
Curator Live Programme
and Outreach
Sonja Borstner: Assistant Curator
Patrizia Dander: Deputy
Director of Curatorial Affairs
Katharina Küster:
Curatorial Editor
Monique Machicao y
Priemer Ferrufino:
Student Assistant

Daniela Medina Poch:
Project Assistant BAUBAU:
A Play Space for Kids
Nadine Nzambisa Ngolo:
Coordination
Education & Outreach
Alexandra Philippovskaya:
Coordination
Education & Outreach
Franka Marlene Schlupp:
Intern Education & Outreach
Elisa Maria Schmitt:
Curatorial Fellow
Paula Vogt: Student Assistant
Christopher Wierling:
Assistant Curator

Exhibition Management

Nora Bergbreiter:
Exhibitions Assistant
Filippa Carlini: Project
Management Exhibitions
Sofia Davydova: Student Assistant
Darina Hashem:
Exhibitions Assistant
Katharina Heise:
Project Management Exhibitions
Elisabeth Pannrucker:
Project Assistant Exhibitions
Simone Schmaus: Head of
Exhibitions and Production
Lisa Tietze: Project
Management Exhibitions
Sophie Winckler: Project
Management Exhibitions

Communications
and Marketing

Nina Benning:
Student Assistant
Paulina Chaimowicz:
Digital Editorial
Ellen Clemens:
Marketing and Events
Greta Diepenbrock:
Student Assistant
Isabel Eberhardt:
Communications Assistant
Matthias Kählert:
Communications Fellow
Luis Kürschner:
Student Assistant
Benicia Mittmann:
Student Assistant
Katrin Mundorf:
Marketing and Education
Birgit Schapow:
Press and Communication
Natalie Schütze: Head of
Communications and
Marketing

Technical Department

Katja Aldinger:
Technical Office Exhibitions
Marc Aldinger:
Technical Office Exhibitions
Steve Bederski:
Technical Office Building
Darina Hashem:
Assistant to Technical Office

André Klose:
Technical Office Building
Dan Leopold: Deputy Head
of Technical Office
André Merfort: Technical
Office Exhibitions
Felix Paul Petzold:
Technical Office Events
Thorsten Seehawer:
Technical Office Building
Bert Schülke: Head
of Technical Office
Thomas Wittmütz:
Technical Office Events
Michael Wolff, Technical Office
Electrical Engineering

Gropius Bau Friends

Umut Azad Akkel, Alina
Amer, Erikas Ingber, Vera Moré,
Petra Petrick, Zorica
Radivojevic-Llalloshi, El Yusser
Sebihi, Veronika Zimmer

Exhibition Maintenance

Onur Agbaba, Lotta Becker,
Kin Man Cheong, Arantxa
Ciafrino, Anne Verena Freybott,
Beatrice Hill-Cai, Paula Ritgen,
Nahomi Wintana Tecle,
Marilyn Nova White

Rirkrit Tiravanija
On Making Less

Published by Bierke Verlag

ISBN 978-3-948546-24-3

The book is published in
parallel in German as
Rirkrit Tiravanija,
Über das Weniger Machen,
ISBN 978-3-948546-23-6

Printing of the excerpts
from Masanobu Fukuoka,
The One-Straw Revolution,
published by New York
Review Books, 2009 (1978),
pp. 15–32, on pp. 59–79,
with kind permission of
© Michiyo Shibuya,
The Fukuoka Estate.

The rights for all slogans,
pp. 15, 57, 93 & 103, are
© Rirkrit Tiravanija

Bierke Verlag
bierke.de

Berliner Festspiele
**GROPIUS
BAU**

Niederkirchnerstraße 7
10963 Berlin
gropiusbau.de

Funded by the German
Federal Cultural Foundation

Funded by the Federal
Government Commissioner
for Culture and the Media

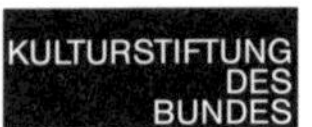

128